A Black Forest Walden

T0244312

SUNY series, Insinuations: Philosophy, Psychoanalysis, Literature

Charles Shepherdson, editor

A Black Forest Walden

Conversations with
Henry David Thoreau and Marlonbrando

DAVID FARRELL KRELL

Back cover image: The author at Walden Pond, near Concord. Photo: Scott Usatorres.

Published by State University of New York Press, Albany

© 2022 State University of New York

All rights reserved

Printed in the United States of America

No part of this book may be used or reproduced in any manner whatsoever without written permission. No part of this book may be stored in a retrieval system or transmitted in any form or by any means including electronic, electrostatic, magnetic tape, mechanical, photocopying, recording, or otherwise without the prior permission in writing of the publisher.

For information, contact State University of New York Press, Albany, NY
www.sunypress.edu

Library of Congress Cataloging-in-Publication Data

Name: Krell, David Farrell, author.
Title: A Black Forest Walden : conversations with Henry David Thoreau and
    Marlonbrando / David Farrell Krell.
Description: Albany : State University of New York Press, [2022] | Series:
    SUNY series, Insinuations : philosophy, psychoanalysis, literature |
    Includes bibliographical references.
Identifiers: LCCN 2021044245 | ISBN 9781438488493 (hardcover : alk. paper) |
    ISBN 9781438488509 (ebook) | ISBN 9781438488486 (pbk. : alk. paper)
Subjects: LCSH: Krell, David Farrell—Homes and haunts—Germany—Black
    Forest. | Thoreau, Henry David, 1817–1862. Walden. | Thoreau, Henry
    David, 1817–1862—Influence. | Marlonbrando (Cat) | Solitude—Germany—Black
    Forest. | Feral cats—Germany—Black Forest. | Human-animal relationships—
    Germany—Black Forest. | Walden Pond (Middlesex County, Mass.)—In
    literature. | Black Forest (Germany)—Biography.
Classification: LCC DD801.B64 K73 2022 | DDC 943/.46—dc23/eng/20211022
LC record available at https://lccn.loc.gov/2021044245

10 9 8 7 6 5 4 3 2 1

for Carol Ann "Buzz" Krell
und für Brigitte, Ingrid, Anne und Joachim Bruns

Contents

Preface

Thoreau—no man has both inspired and irritated me more. That's me speaking here, but it could as easily have been Emerson or a dozen others who shared their lives with Thoreau, who was an inspiration, an irritation, and a royal—no, a *democratic*—thorn in the side.

During the mid-1990s, I had the chance to occupy a ski cabin in the Black Forest region of Germany, south of Freiburg, north of Basel, Switzerland, and close to the Rhine River and French Alsace. From 2009 on, I was able to live here permanently, thanks to the generosity of Brigitte Bruns and her family. My experiences here brought me into conversation with Thoreau and with Marlonbrando—a feral cat whom I fed regularly, although he had no need of it, and who came to serve as a kind of therapist for me. A tough one.

I began writing these aphorisms before the start of the present millennium. Important phases of rewriting or new writing came in 2006, 2012, 2016, and 2021. Bibliographical and explanatory notes appear at the end of the book, either indicating my sources or giving an account of some not-so-evident reference or matter at hand. Also at the end of the book is a list of illustrations, which offers a series of captions for the photos. All but one of these photos—a snapshot taken by an unknown person not long after the cabin was built—are my own, a small sample of the thousands I have taken over the years.

A Black Forest Walden is dedicated to my sister "Buzz," aka Carol Ann Krell, who through all the phases of my life has been a guide to me and a heart's friend, and to Brigitte Bruns and her family, the owners of "my" cabin. My thanks to the generous readers of the manuscript of this book, to my sponsoring editor at SUNY Press Rebecca Colesworthy, to the production editor Jenn Bennett-Genthner, to the copy editor Sue Kauffman, to the compositor and designer of the book Susan Morreale, and to Charles Shepherdson, editor of the "Insinuations" series. I can still hear Charles reciting from memory the entire prologue to *The Canterbury Tales* one warm summer evening on the terrace of a villa near Perugia, Italy. Decades have flown since then, but I will never forget his extraordinary declamation, in impeccable Middle English, of that great poem.

D. F. K.

Strobelhütte, St. Ulrich

1

Silent snowfall

It happens over and over again throughout the winter, so why does it always surprise me? The evening, all windstorm, soon passes over into a night of rainfall. Droplets dance on the metal roof of the cabin—lightly, on their toes, and I doze; heavily, foot stomping, and I stir. Then silence. I sleep. In the morning, a lambent white light fills the bedroom of the cabin. The mirror affixed to the door of the old cupboard at the head of my bed tells me what I already know. I rise and gaze out the window at Douglas the Fir. His branches strain under the weight of white. The fields stretching up to Schauinsland Mountain blaze white-hot with cold. It's always the same feeling that accompanies the first overwhelming glimpse of snowfall at the cabin, the feeling of having been hoodwinked during the night, the sense that I should have known what the night—that inexpressibly beautiful creature—was up to, or down to. The Snow Queen of Kurosawa's *Dreams* has once again suffocated me softly in the night, and once again I awake in paradise.

The colors of snow; or, where beauty is

When Monet and Pissarro paint snow, it is all roses and bluebells with an orange aura and a crimson afterglow—every color but white. Of course, white isn't a color at all, but, as we learned in school, it is all the colors spun around on a disc. That spinning disc is rarely encountered out there in the world, to be sure, but painted snow teaches us the lesson anyway. Herman Melville calls white "the colorless all-color," and so it is, even at night, under a moon.

Years ago, I arrived at the cabin with a lover. We were jet lagged and could not sleep during the night. We sensed, then saw, in the moonlight outside the cabin window that snow had fallen. We got up, dressed, and stepped out the cabin door into two feet of snow. It was four o'clock in the morning. The waxing moon was only half full, but it lit up the blanketed valley. We walked, or trudged, in silence over Edward's Heights until dawn. In the black of night, under moonlight, the snow crystals glittered violet

and green—amethyst and sapphire—with each laborious step of ours. With each turn of the head or inclination of the back and shoulders, the snow scintillated in alternating flashes of green and purple, purple and green, each more brilliant than the last. It was as though not white but purple-green was the all-color. A flashing round dance of vert and violet seemed to capture the entire spectrum of colors, including ultraviolet and infrared. The philosopher Friedrich Joseph Schelling calls the unity of violet and green "supreme splendor," and we believed him. We returned to the cabin, cooked a big breakfast, made love, slept away the day, and woke to another night of moonlit snow. We discovered that lag can also make a life.

Since then, I have walked over Edward's Heights under snow and moonlight many times, searching for amethyst and sapphire but finding only diamonds. On these later occasions, I was alone. That was how I learned that vert and violet had been effluences of her eyes, and that beauty is in the eye of the beholder's beloved.

3

In the still of the night

If recently you've been living in a city, your first night in the cabin can be disconcerting, no matter how happy you are to get there. (You get there by taking a tram through Freiburg from the railway station to the southern outskirts of town, catching a bus up to the most remote village—the bus leaves once every hour till nightfall—then walking up the steepest hill on the horizon off to your right, Barley Stalk Hill, about a ninety-minute walk.)

Disconcerting first of all because of the chill in the walls. Whether winter or summer, the cabin walls are cold and damp long after you light your first fire. In winter, it will take you three days' and nights' worth of fires to rout that chill, even if the forester has come early on the day of your arrival (he has a key) and lit a fire for you. In summer, the chill will be banished more quickly once you light your fire and open all the windows and the door.

Disconcerting in the second place because even after your bed is warm on that first night (ah, the featherbed! we will have to come back to this little touch of heaven!) so that you drift off into a grateful and gratifying sleep, you will be roused in the middle of the night by something else—the stillness.

Absolute silence is like noise: you can hear it. You wake up and you listen to it. You rise and fall on its waves, its periods and cadences. It fills your ears like the chirpings of tinnitus, and you wonder at it. You do not hear the man in the moon breathing, because he does not breathe. Yet in the silence you sense him looking at you, and you feel his pull on the seas and the blood. The stillness is palpable. Sometimes it is so disquieting that you have to rise and go outside to see if it is real, or if the cabin has become a pyramid. Once outside, you feel the winter wind or summer breeze, and more important, you hear it in the trees. After a while the silence abates, goes quiet. You can go back to bed now.

Back in Chicago or New York City, the drunken brawl outside your window has to escalate to beer bottle smashing or a gunfire exchange before you hear it. Here, the stillness of the night escalates without police or ambulance sirens, without cries and whispers or sound and fury, and it has all the time in the world to wait until you hearken to it. You will.

4

The snowplow

The roar of a motor at night—what can it be but the destroyer of sleep? It is true that whenever the salt-strewing snowplow comes bellowing up the switchback asphalt road of the Möhlin Valley, all the way up to the parking lot that is located several hundred meters south and east of the cabin, I wake up. Sleep is suspended, at least for a few moments, until the plow clears the parking area of snow, turns, and heads back down the road. Yet I am always delighted, no matter how heavy with sleep my head may be. I open my eyes to the brilliant headlights lighting up the forest pines and the spinning orange warning lights whose beams turn up periodically in the mirror. They are like searchlights in the sky near an airport or the beam of the outermost lighthouse. Nothing makes me feel more secure or gives me more hope for the day to come, not because I have anywhere to go, but simply because of the company. Depending on the timing of the snow or ice storm, the truck may come chugging by at one or three or five o'clock in the morning: the drivers do not sleep all winter long, no hibernation for them. It isn't that I'm grateful for their work. For years now, I have been hoping to be snowed in for weeks at a time, to be like Jack in that high Colorado hotel laboring diligently over his book, all work and no play. And every year the undaunted, unstoppable snowplow frustrates my hope. I should be growling. Yet there is something reassuring about the deep hum of the engine and the scrape of the plow, as there is about a lonesome freight train's whistle in the night. There is a world out there, a world of workers and wanderers, and it sings to me like Woody Guthrie or Pete Seeger, "Go to sleep, you weary hobo, let the towns drift slowly by." So I turn and scrunch the featherbed tight around my shoulder and know that there is a world in here too. And mine is appreciably warmer.

Ice wings

"Many of the phenomena of Winter are suggestive of an inexpressible tenderness and fragile delicacy. We are accustomed to hear this king described as a rude and boisterous tyrant; but with the gentleness of a lover he adorns the tresses of Summer." So says Henry David Thoreau (W 234), and he is right. If the dense fog lasts through the night and Boreas the north wind blows lightly but steadily till dawn, each twig and tine of the leafless birch on the meadow above the cabin forms along its entire length a wing of transparent ice an inch or more in width. By morning, the tree is an enormous white bird or, when the wind blows, a musical instrument. The poet Georg Trakl calls these ice wings *crystalline angels*.

There is a clearing near the edge of the forest on Barley Stalk Hill. Stinging nettles flourish there in summer, growing chest high in the rich soil. The very sight of them on a summer morning sets the skin to tingling. In winter, the tall stalks are stripped of their nettlesome leaves. The ice wings construct an enchanting heaven out of their little hell; they are swaying seraphim rather than stinging satans. A few meters farther on, huge boughs of pine and fir dip under the weight of ice wings grown so close together—crowding every needle and branch—that they form something like tufts of thick white wool, a warm mantle of ice, winter fur for winter firs—but back to that solitary birch on the meadow.

When the March sun burns off the frozen fog, usually by mid-afternoon, the wings take flight, an Icarus of ice, and plunge to the ground. A silhouette of shattered wings, shards of iced fog, spreads across the matted brown grass beneath the tree. Within half an hour every wing has fallen, the music is stilled, and the naked birch grows taciturn once again. It wants to bud leaves, not ice wings. I scoop up some jagged fragments of ice and hold their freeze, albeit only for a melting moment. I notice that the wings are ribbed, as though for tensile strength, testifying to the long and patient labors of the night fog. But did any effort at all go into these formations? One tree would have taken you and me years of work to transform. So much effort! No effort at all for nature. The fragments chill my palm, then swell to one great tear that rolls across my lifeline, uncertain of the cause of its weeping. Toil? Time? Warmth? Transient beauty?

6

The Storm Beech

The enormous tree, my most august neighbor, dominates the hill and the sky of the pasture above the cabin. In fact, the sky stretches over the Storm Beech like a tarpaulin, gray in winter, blue in summer; the beech's roots gather together the earth, frozen and brown in winter, green and gay with wildflowers in summer. It is called the Storm Beech because the south wind has shaped it for a century or two, twisting and bending its boughs so that they incline toward the northeast like the myriad needles of numberless compasses. "No tree has so fair a bole and so handsome an instep as the beech," says Thoreau in an unpublished text cited by Ralph Waldo Emerson (SW 428). On every fair summer evening, I sit on that instep—one of the many insteps, which are the thick gray roots almost entirely exposed to the light and air. Onto one of the neighboring insteps, one that happens to be flattened and scarred, I place my wine cup. The blood of the grape is sometimes red, sometimes pale yellow-green, and I toast the setting sun after it has toasted me during the day. I lay back in the arms of the tree and study—through gnarled branches and a riot of green leaves—the brilliant sky. The great beech has soaked up so much caloric during the day that it now communicates it to me: if I am able to write tomorrow, it will be thanks to the energy transfer from tree to me.

One of the locals told me many years ago about the arboreal energy of the Storm Beech, but I was skeptical at the time and merely laughed: old wives' tales. As I toast the sun now, I do not forget to salute the Storm Beech, which extends over me its protecting boughs and leaves and subtends me with its earth-embracing root system. I may be dendritically drunk. Or perhaps I have gone a bit mad, tetched by numerous old wives and their stories? Am I altogether a beechnut?

The Moon and Venus

I had to catch the first bus to Freiburg on a December morning and so had to leave the cabin at five o'clock, long before daylight. The chilly sky blinked with iced stars. The waning moon showed but a sliver, even though I could easily make out the shadowy circle or corona of the entire sphere. It was like an eclipse of the sun, with the curved arc of the celestial body startlingly clear, as though backlit. Below the moon was the brightest satellite I had ever seen, huge and silver and seemingly unmoving. It could not have been a manmade satellite, yet I had never seen the likes of it before. Had the calendar put us closer to Christmas, I would have thought of Bethlehem, Hallmark, and Monty Python. A friend later told me it was Saturn, vast enough on its own, yet appearing even larger because of its rings. No earthling could make out the rings, of course, but I was witness to a massive, unified, argentine light in the black sky, immobile beneath a melon slice of moon. Silver beneath sliver, a celestial calembour, at which I stared for many minutes, standing stock-still beneath the boughs of the gigantic Storm Beech, so that I had to hurry through the dark woods and down the mountain in order not to miss my bus.

Later I discovered that the brilliant satellite beneath the moon was in fact not ringed Saturn but naked Venus, the Morning Star, a mere thirty-five million miles off and thus more intimate with Earth than she normally is. Saturn was off scowling in some other portion of the heavens, probably looking for Venus. Venus Aphrodite, without rings, hoops, or girdles, stood at the center of the vortex and radiated outward to every god and every mortal in her stunning nudity. I should have known.

The cabin; or, plucking the raisins

It doesn't belong to me, but friends have made the cabin available to me for decades now. I came here two or three times a year, as the university calendar allowed, and I came for longer stays if I was lucky enough to get a sabbatical or a grant. Now that I am retired, I live here year-round. That is one thing Thoreau and I have in common: I am as big a bum as he ever was, making leisure and even indolence my profession, reading and writing when I should be doing real work in the real world. The right-wing politicians are so grateful to have me! I am as useless as they are, except that they get to rowel up the public against me.

—Lock up the lazy professor! Elect the lazy populist!

It is true that I lead a privileged life. The French philosopher Maurice Merleau-Ponty confessed near the end of his days that he had been lucky enough to practice his avocation as his profession, and so it has been for me. I've done a bit of work along the way, and, as it turns out, reading and writing have been essential to that work. Whereas the vast majority of men and women have to work at a job, however, I have always been able to make the job work for my avocation. Yet I react ambivalently to Thoreau's bragging about his autonomy and economic independence: on the one hand, I cannot match his vaunted self-reliance, and on the other, I don't want to try. For there is something disingenuous about such declarations of autonomy—which may be nothing more than self-deception. For Thoreau, as for me, there is a social network that keeps us from bumping our heads too hard against reality. For millions of US-Americans, past and present, that social network has ten-foot gaps between each strand of the net, plenty of space for human beings to fall through and crack their skulls and discover that absolutely no one cares. It isn't merely that Thoreau and I can dine at Emerson's whenever our own cupboard is bare or that a solicitous aunt will go our bail: it's that the net is in every respect tighter for the privileged—and the privileged are us.

And so, privileged, I came here as often as I could—to Sankt Ulrich in the Black Forest. The cabin occupies a secluded spot at the edge of the woods on the highest hill hereabouts, at the top of the valley. It takes me about an hour to walk down to the village and the ancient church. The monks arrived here from Cluny in 1025, and when they arrived, they encountered a few farms sprinkled across the broad, steeply ascending valley. Not much in the valley seems to have changed since, and yet Sankt Ulrich, like the rest of the world, is altogether different from the way it was. That is a contradiction, I know. Yet the world is big, and contains multitudes.

A store-owning couple from Freiburg built the cabin in the late 1920s as a weekend retreat and retirement nest. They lived here into ripe old age. The woods were sparser then, and there were more hayfields. It is an ironic development: the forest arrogates more and more of the valley to itself as acid rain, global warming, and ravenous beetles threaten each tree in it. The people of the village too are threatened. With each passing year, more and more of the young people give up on the valley and its agriculture and move to the city, where the trades or professions they practice take them. Fewer and fewer farmers keep the number of cows and pigs and chickens they used to keep. They don't have the helping hands anymore, and they are getting old. Besides, agribusiness seems destined to undersell them, with animals pumped up on hormones and antibiotics and fed on male chick feed and cattle bonemeal laced with the mad cow disease. That's progress. People around here don't like to think too much about economy: the prospects are short term, and the phrase one hears repeatedly is disconsolate.

—*Es rendiert sich nicht mehr.* (It's no longer viable. It doesn't pay.)

Short-term prospects prevail, except for the prospect from my perch at the top of the valley—the prospect of a parasite, to be sure, but a grateful one. I can see Schauinsland Mountain from the cabin window on the east, and if the great bald pate of Belchen Mountain didn't obstruct my view to the south, I could see all the way to the Swiss Alps. Even the local farmers, when they visit me, comment on the prospect.

—You've picked the most beautiful spot in the valley. You have the emperor's view.

They are right, even if politically incorrect.

Seen from the outside, the cabin is a modest two-story structure, a typical Schwarzwald house, just tinier than most. Above the concrete skirting that surrounds the half-cellar, which contains the water pump and tribes of wintering or summering field mice, the thick walls of stone are cladded with cedar shingles. The east and south walls are interrupted by generous double windows on both the first and second floors, each window framed by heavy wooden shutters painted (what else?) forest green. The most remarkable feature of the cabin, however, is the metal roof: its welded steel plates, painted a dark brown, protect me from the elements but also regale me with an incredible symphony of sound every time it rains, to say nothing of the hailstorms.

Inside, a tiny entrance hall opens onto the small kitchen (to the right), the surprisingly modern bathroom (to the left, added to the structure in the 1960s), and the old-fashioned living room or *stube* (straight ahead). The *stube* is warmed by a tile stove, fed from the kitchen, which heats every room in the house except the bathroom. (In the modern bathroom, electricity saves the shivering timbers and the shivering bather.) To feed the tile oven, I gather pine boughs and branches from my own woods. These branches of white and red pine, spruce, larch, and Douglas Fir make the best fires: the branches are as hard as the knots they form on the main trunk. As the trunk grows higher in the sky and greater in girth each year, the side branches (*Bengel*, they are called—*Tannenbengel*) grow increasingly compact and hard. You can't *start* a fire with them. You need to chop some thin pine chips for starters, but you can keep the fire going wonderfully well with them. So much, for the moment, about "vital heat," which is one of Thoreau's favorite economic subjects, and one of mine too. A cabin in the woods will do that to you, sometimes in July as much as in January. But to return to the *stube* or parlor.

A large cherry wood table for eating and for writing dominates the room. It is fitted into the L-shaped window seat that extends along the east and south walls just beneath the windows. A plush sofa, covered in burgundy-colored velvet, graces the north wall; above the sofa, shelves of books and CDs. The west wall, which separates the *stube* from the

kitchen, consists mostly of the cream-colored tiles of the stove. Although the stube is tiny, you can seat six almost comfortably, but in any case intimately, around the table. A wooden bench skirts the tile stove—in German, *Kachelofen*—and when you come in out of the snow there is nothing more delightful than plopping down on the bench and leaning back onto the piping hot tiles. *Almost* nothing more delightful. For the best method is to pour yourself a thimbleful of schnapps before you plop down; that way, you heat inside and outside simultaneously. Around here schnapps is called "central heating."

The southeast corner of the stube, catty-corner from the entrance, is the Lord God's Corner, *Herrgotteswinkel*, preserved even in my pagan household. In earlier days, the dead were laid out on the window seat with their heads beneath the crucifix of the *Herrgotteswinkel*, but I doubt the cabin is old enough to have seen that ritual: in Freiburg there have long been hospitals with back doors and mortuaries with front doors. Assorted photographs of prior inhabitants grace the corner shelf beneath the cross, which has a doily and votive candles, too. Indeed, it is a kind of altar to the Penates, with a framed *Huus-Spruch* (house poem) composed in the Alemannic dialect and written in splendid calligraphy. The first two stanzas of this *Huus-Spruch*, composed for his new neighbors by Hubert Baum, author of the Alemannic dictionary, give an idea of the whole:

> *Guet im Stai*
> *Satt im Holz*
> *Groß un Chlai*
> *Hüet I stolz.*
> *Im e Fründ*
> *Gib I Rueh*
> *Vor d' Fiind*
> *Beschließ I zue.*

> Firm-footed in stone
> Wood strong and wide
> Folk large and small
> I shield with pride.
> If it's a friend
> I grant a peaceful night
> Before an enemy
> I shut my door tight.

A photograph taken fifty years after they built the cabin shows the old couple framed in a window: he is skinny, with hunched shoulders, arthritic fingers, and large flaps of ears; she is stockier, with deep-set eyes; both are smiling broadly, both still full of life. They could have been my *Opa* (grandfather) and *Oma* (grandmother).

It is difficult—no, impossible—for me to think of Germany in the thirties and forties, when these two, the first inhabitants, were in their prime. I am obligated to remember, however, and so I persist at it. My own paternal grandfather and grandmother arrived in the United States at the turn of the twentieth century. They were raising their children during the First World War and playing with their grandchildren during the Second. Their own people were from Alsace, across the Rhine, an hour's drive into France from here. From its high perch, the cabin saw the worst happen—during the Third Reich and the war. It must have been confused and horrified, for it is a place of welcome and shelter, at least to me.

There are two bedrooms on the second floor. You get to them by means of a foldaway ladder or steep set of stairs in the entrance hall. Never descend the stairs facing front, unless you are in a hurry and careless of how gravity will get you down. The interior of both stories is clad in dark-stained pine, *satt im Holz*, as the house poem says, the tongue-and-groove boards still largely straight and well joined. The cabin itself is clean and orderly, restful to the eyes. If there is clutter on the shelves, it is because so many folks with different kinds of needs—needs ranging from Chinese sticks to playing cards to philosophy books—have lived here. One upstairs bedroom is tiny: a six-footer sleeps with head and feet against the walls, like a temporary support beam. The larger bedroom holds a large bed arranged against the north and east walls of the house. If you were to sleep against the south wall, you would be the first to be informed of oncoming storms bursting through the Burgundian Gate. The large window on the east wall opens onto the swaying branches of Douglas the Fir, who towers over the cabin. A mammoth tree, Douglas welcomes the snow in winter and in summer sponsors choruses of birds.

A German acquaintance of mine from Frankfurt, hearing how I lived, felt he had to chastise me.

—You're spoiled. Your life up there is like plucking the raisins out of the shit.

Unfortunately, that is a common German expression. He clearly wanted me to eat unplucked filth like everybody else in Frankfurt. He was a philosopher doing research on social justice; I was a philosopher doing research on envy and ressentiment.

9

The past has not passed

Of course, the Frankfurter has a point, envy or no. There is so much in the world at present that cries for change, so much in the past that weeps because it cannot change. Friedrich Nietzsche says that our will shatters against the little phrase, "It *was*." If I travel to a new part of Germany and I learn that there is a death camp nearby, I never fail to go to it. One walks in silence there, brain and senses numbed, attentive to every detail and yet blinded by it all, and then one leaves. Transformed? Different, in any case. The best way to remember is never to memorialize. Time itself then becomes the past of a future—a recurrent "It *was*"—that will never pass or be passed by.

10

Neighbors

I do not mean the goats and cows, who are my real neighbors, my closest, ever-present, ever-cheering neighbors, but other living creatures in my vicinity. I'll offer portraits of a few of them in the pages that follow, starting with Franz.

I call Franz "Saint Francis" because he talks to his animals, and they talk back to him. Politely, for the most part. Out on the steep pastures above his house, Franz has Scottish Highlanders, with their Texas Longhorn long horns and their shaggy Scots coats. Not the usual breed of kine hereabouts.

He has every sort of duck and goose from around the world in his pond. Even his sheep are oddly disparate. He lives at the other edge of the forest about a kilometer away from me, and the bees he keeps swarm among the pines and firs there. Whenever rainfall is plentiful and spring temperatures are propitious, a certain louse chews on the sap exuded by the conifers, and the bees feed on what the lice excrete, plucking the raisins, as it were, to produce honey. It is only out of delicacy and not out of an intent to deceive that the apiarists hereabouts, Franz included, label their product Pine Tree Honey rather than Nectar of Louse Shit. Isn't nature wonderful! Especially when it is spruced up by culture!

As for Saint Francis, don't be fooled: when a fox persisted in supping on his ducks and geese, Franz grabbed his flintlock and sent the fox to feral heaven, as Thoreau would have wanted him to. If, unlike the fox, you are gentle with his beasts and show respect, you will find Franz the kindest and most agreeable of your neighbors, with amiable laughter bubbling on his lips. As for the proverbial twinkle in the eye, Franz invented it. Finally, a word to the gustatorily wise: Franz's nectar of louse shit is food for the gods.

11

But where's the pond?

Sankt Ulrich lacks a large body of water. Everywhere up here we come across gurgling streams, sparkling brooks alive with tadpoles and tiny trout: rivulets leap and twist at every turn, rushing down the valley's hillsides till they find the Rhine. Trout ponds have been secreted away in this or that corner of the woods. Yet there is no large pond, much less a lake. We lack the transcendentalist's celestial eye here; we cannot see the sky reflected perfectly on an imperfect earth. "It is well to have some water in your neighborhood, to give buoyancy and to float the earth" (W 64), says Thoreau, and once again he is right. He gets up early and bathes in Walden Pond, his testicles shrinking to tiny purple plums—he does not mention this detail, but one can surmise it. Bathing is for him a ritual, as it was for the ballsier Whitman.

I too used to practice this ritual when I lived near the shore of Lake Michigan north of Chicago. I remember the first foolhardy sallies into the lake in June. Already the air was warm, even at five-thirty in the morning, but the water was wintry. My calves would tighten and start to ache, and I would turn and limp a hasty retreat. Yet I'd be back the next morning, and the day after that, trying to go out a bit farther each day until testes and tête could take the punishment. In full summer out in the lake you could dive to the bottom and, looking up, watch the sun emerge on the watery horizon, shimmering and bobbing on the windy surface of the lake. As long as you started the day with that cosmic vision, the day itself could bring whatever chicanery it liked. I remember the last mornings in mid-October, when the morning air was more than brisk but the water still summer warm, at least until the Canadian current swept down the lake (Blame Canada! Blame Canada!), and my calves were too proud to concede defeat: once again, I surface dove—against my better judgment—and felt my skull split right down the middle. How wrenching it was for me to walk away from the water on that last day, leaving my body and my hopes behind, with nothing to cheer me but the onslaught of the Chicago winter.

No, Sankt Ulrich has no lake and no ponds for people. And one does not bathe in the streams, winter or summer. One longs for a lake in August, a lake or an ocean, and one dreams of the Aegean Sea. There is plenty of water to drink, of course. At every turn of the dirt path or gravel road you will find a trough—a giant hollow log fed by a slender trunk of pine grooved along its length and carrying water to the trough from the fern-draped spring. In summer, you splash fresh water on your face and the nape of your neck and drink from your numb cupped palms. In winter, you crack the gnarled ice if you can and drink directly from the grooved stem. Even in August the water is freezing cold and absolutely pristine. You can't drink too much of it—it is too cold—but you can certainly slake your thirst for the time it takes to reach the next trough.

Some of the loveliest woods hereabouts are in the area called *Kaltwasser* (cold water). There is a Cold Water Farm as well, although it has cows and chickens, too. When you pass through the pasture and enter the cool shadow of the forest, the stream flows quietly along on your left. The water there is black, or seems to be, because of the shadows and the bed of sable silt and decayed beech leaves. In March, a galaxy of tadpoles drifts in this black stream. They are almost impossible to see once they have freed themselves from the transparent jelly egg sack. When you bend over to get a better look at them, the tadpoles wriggle their way under a protecting leaf or bore into the silt like ostriches. What becomes of them all? You certainly do not hear a million frogs quacking throughout the summer months. I do not know. But the birds in that portion of the wood are remarkably chubby.

Here in the Black Forest the water seems to be more deeply interfused with the earth than at Thoreau's Walden Pond. Here we find, not Thoreau's rippled, glassy, specular sky water, but downward flowing earth water. Thoreau's pond in general is more transcendently and transcendentally spiritual than anything here can be, even though Germany is the fabled home of poets and philosophers. Thoreau writes of Walden Pond:

> A field of water betrays the spirit that is in the air. It is continually receiving new life and motion from above. It is intermediate in its nature between land and sky. On land only the grass and trees wave, but the water itself is rippled by the wind. I see where the breeze dashes across it by the streaks or flakes of light. It is remarkable that we can look down on its surface. We shall, perhaps, look down thus on the surface of air at length, and mark where a still subtler spirit sweeps over it. (W 143)

Precisely because he writes here of surfaces and of looking down, one can see that Thoreau's trajectory is always ascensional, gliding ever upward to the most rarefied ethers. Here, in the Schwarzwald, the water hugs the earth and plunges as the valley descends to the Rhine Plain. Here, the water seeps from mossy rocks and dribbles down the verdant bank. It loves to hide. You put your nose into the redolent moss, and you get wet. That is how you find the subtler pond. That is how your thought should be. Descensional.

12

River of fog

I was walking up the path at Barley Stalk Hill on a crystalline winter morning after having fetched my milk. Barley Stalk Hill is shaped like a saddle on the crest of the hill, with two forested knolls on either side of it. You can spot it from miles away. The knoll on the left is called the *Galgenkopf* (Gallows' Head), so called because a certain civic ritual used to be carried out there; the knoll on the right, where I have my "office," is the *Hörnli* (Little Horn). Not the Little Big Horn. In between these two knolls, each thick with pine, larch, and spruce, sits the deep saddle of swayback Barley Stalk Hill. As I was climbing the path toward the lowest point on the saddle, at its center, a river of lavender fog came pouring over

the horizon and slowly, almost imperceptibly, engulfed me. It had been a brilliant winter morning, the snowy hills leaping into the blinding blue sky, but now the day was lost to me, or I to it.

Why lavender? Because of the cerulean backdrop, I suppose. I do not know whether fog normally has a color, but up on Barley Stalk Hill, I have bathed in its smoky lavender river.

My "office"

Decades before the cabin became available to me, there was a spot in the woods above it that invited me on summer mornings and did not release me until the evening. A plush carpet of moss grows over the rocks there, and it stays amazingly dry in spite of all the rainfall. I shift from office chair to office chair during the day, reading or writing whatever has to be read or written. I stretch my legs from time to time on a lazy perambulation among the gigantic pines, then settle back to work. For entertainment and companionship I place a shiny object or a sheet of paper on the ground at my side: the monarchs flutter down onto it, staying sometimes for an hour or so, drying their wings or simply being gorgeous. Perhaps they are interested in my writing and are reading over my shoulder, so to speak?

I have always sensed that the only angels there ever were—apart from Trakl's crystalline variety—are animals, wild animals, so that there are still angels galore, even as an encroaching civilization systematically snuffs them out. I remember a summer day when my daughter Elena Sophia, then a senior in high school, was visiting the "office." She was working on a research paper on Abraham Lincoln while I was trying to write a screenplay. We worked quietly for hours, she sitting with her back abutting a pine, I on one of the mossy office chairs facing her. I heard a faint rustling sound and looked up. A young doe was grazing behind the tree, unaware of the presence of humans, who are usually noisy. I signaled to Elena, made a hush sign, and pointed behind her tree, giving her the eye sign so that she would look. She leaned far to her left, gazing around the girth of the tree. At that precise instant, the doe raised her head and looked directly into my daughter's eyes. Such a meeting of deer eyes on both sides—big, brown, radiant, and astonished—has never occurred before or since. The doe held the gaze for an eternity of seconds, then backed slowly away.

Even during the winter months, I stop in at my office every now and then just to make sure that all is running smoothly. The moss peeks through the snow and invites me to take a seat. Come June, I'll accept the invitation.

Conversations with Marlon Brando?

Well, actually, with Marlonbrando, the cat. He's not really my cat. He's a feral feline who haunts and hunts the fields around the cabin. I began to feed him during the winter months to make a favorable impression on the tribes of mice in the cabin cellar and walls. Marlonbrando was a daily visitor for about fifteen years.

It all started with a November storm. The wind wanted to blow the cabin off the hilltop clear to the next village, but the cabin demurred and held fast. I was enjoying my supper and a glass of pinot noir from nearby Alsace when a gray cat with a large white patch on its chest hopped up onto the outside windowsill. It was clearly seeking shelter from the storm. It? I mean *he*, Marlonbrando. Yet as soon as I made a move to open the window so that the critter could come inside, he leapt from the sill down onto the chopping block below. I had to learn distance and discretion. And so I filled a bowl with food scraps and a drinking cup with water, placed them on the sill, and closed the window tight. He learned to recognize the sound of the window latch closing, which became a sort of Pavlov's bell for him. Once he heard its reassuring click, he would leap back up onto the sill. Marlonbrando was not exactly the trusting type, not exactly your sentimental lap cat. And not exactly an angel, either.

How did I know it was Marlonbrando and not Umathurman? Because of the size of his head. And because he sprayed the window before he left on that first night, leaving me a sort of bouquet and all competing felines a warning. Umathurman would have left dreamier waftings.

At every supper hour throughout the winter and spring, Marlonbrando would leap onto the sill from the chopping block below and creep across to his bowl of cat food (with occasional scraps from the plate of the master of the house) and his cup of water. Before he commenced the repast, however, he would turn his great golden eyes toward me. He was fascinated by the candles I always had burning to make the lonely supper table more festive, the flames of his eyes meeting the paraffin-fed flames of the candles. Then he would look up into my own far less furious eyes, whereupon I would raise my glass:

—Marlonbrando!

He said nothing, at least at first, but only turned his head and bolted down his food. I felt that he would eventually mellow. I believed that by April he would be in my lap.

At long last, after many evenings and countless bowls of chow, he began to respond to my salutations and toastings. Yet he wasn't exactly gregarious, nor certainly in any obvious way grateful.

—It's only a matter of size, you know, he murmured one night to my amazement.

—How's that?

—A matter of size, you and me.

His grammar was not good.

—What do you mean, a matter of size?

—The difference between us. Size . . . and this pane of glass.

—I don't understand.

—I think you do. I'm sure you do. Look into my eyes. Try to look deep.

—What are you, a hypnotist?

—You see? You cannot look into my eyes, because they are all surface, like this pane of glass. I don't get into your house, you don't get into mine.

I rose and started for the window, thinking that I had been a churlish host and that he wanted in; he spun and crouched, ready to pounce back onto the chopping block. I froze.

—All right, all right. I'll stay where I am. Come back and finish your supper.

I resumed my place at the table and began to eat again. He looked about in every direction, came slowly out of his crouch, and returned to his bowl. We remained taciturn until, at length, I broke the silence. In spite of the window, I did not have to shout: he could hear me through the double pane of glass with a single twitch of his ear.

—You sure are a nervous critter.

—It's only a matter of size, he snapped.

It was the only time he ever snapped at me. His replies were normally calm and considered, his aperçus the result of a thinking process that took its time. I do not mean that he was slow. Measured, rather.

—Size, yours and mine, he said again, this time more equably. If I were a bit larger—and we're not talking monstrous, just a little bit larger— our situations would be reversed, you know.

—Reversed?

—You wouldn't be having me for supper. I would be having you.

I laughed at his joke, even though I knew he'd stolen it from a movie he'd seen. Now I waited for him to tell me he "coulda been a contenda" But he didn't make jokes, and he didn't laugh. From the mirror surface of his gold-glazed gazing eyes, I could feel him sizing me up—my physical size, my moral stature, the full spread of my courage and will to survive. It did not take him long.

He bolted down the rest of his munchies and then himself bolted. Every evening it was the same. He looked back at me as he sauntered up the path, licking his chops. It wasn't to say thank you, this parting glance. Marlonbrando was not so effusive.

—Seeyaround.

15

Ice wings, Part Two

Hoarfrost is universal because fog is an all-embracing atmosphere. Last night the gentle breeze shifted, coming out of the south rather than the north, bringing a lot of moisture with it. Yet the air was already so bitter cold that ice wings formed on the sides of every object. That is what you notice about ice wings: the perfection, the pervasiveness, the absolute rule. Your eye, following the line of the goat fence, with its four-by-six-inch rectangles

formed by wire now clad in purest white—not simply the regular strands of wire but every wispy stray, from excess curl of wire to splinter of wooden post to gossamer spider web—obeying the imperious yet utterly silent command to display the perfection. It is not symmetry, not the bland uniformity of identity, but cosmic perfection nonetheless. They used to tell us that each snowflake is different from every other—that was the Snowflake Proof for the Existence of God, and every flake was convinced by it. No, neither symmetry nor uniformity nor identity, but the overwhelming embrace of an eminently adaptable, all-gathering and all-differentiating white. For the ice wings I have seen today, myriad needles of varying lengths and thicknesses of frozen frost, stand side by side and hold hands all around: an Alban confederation of matchless individuals proud in the sun.

16

Douglas the Fir

In an old photograph taken at about the time the cabin was built, Douglas is a mere Christmas tree, and one of only two trees in the vicinity. Now, a century later, he towers over the larches, beeches, birches, spruce, cherry, and mountain ash at the eastern end of the cabin. (The front entrance faces west; the two big windows of the stube, as I mentioned, face south and east.) His most impressive aspect is from my bedroom window when I am gazing in the direction of Schauinsland Mountain. The lower boughs are themselves as thick as tree trunks. One of these boughs bends upward like a ballerina's arm, its hand and fingers extending elegantly over the roof of the cabin. When snow presses the fingers downward, they tap on the steel roof, and the cabin becomes a conga drum. When the snow melts, the rhythm of the ploppings is irregular but always musical.

Douglas is of course ever green. He adds a touch of immutability to the seasons. And the fragrance of his needles is potent and sweet: citrus—oranges and lemons—rather than pine. Red pine smells like turpentine, but white pine and Douglas are fruit baskets. No matter how far you wander from the cabin in the direction of Schauinsland, you can spot Douglas. He looms. He rules. He's the Jolly Green Giant calling you home for supper.

17

Aurora

What can you say in defense of a man who likes to get out of bed before first light so that he can be awake for the rising of the sun? Whatever you may say, you will say it of both Henry David and this David. We both love the auroral, the glow of the dawn in all things. I once loved a woman who said that there is nothing more depressing than a sunrise. There are, they say, evening people and morning people. When I was young, I too was of the evening's party, the party of the night. I'm not sure when that changed, although the alteration seems to have coincided with the arrival of my three children. Themselves creatures of the night, three sweet Draculas, they helped transform me into a daylight monster. Thoreau too loves the mornings, wants the morning to stretch all the way to suppertime. Not that he wants to *do* anything with his mornings. None of that early-to-bed-early-to-rise twaddle for Henry. He wants those early morning hours to last so that he can "make a day of it" (W 72), as he says, for no other reason than to know that he is alive. Thoreau is an auroral vagabond, a penny loafer treading the dewy paths of morning. Whereas I love to fill my mornings with projects and purposefulness, Thoreau loves to warm the doorstep with his butt. "Rapt in a reverie," he says (W 83). Here is one of the most beautiful passages in *Walden*, and one of the most important for me, even though, ultimately, I cannot do what it enjoins:

> There were times when I could not afford to sacrifice the bloom of the present moment to any work, whether of the head or hands. I love a broad margin to my life. Sometimes, in a summer morning, having taken my accustomed bath, I sat in my sunny doorway from sunrise till noon, rapt in a revery, amidst the pines the hickories and sumachs, in undisturbed solitude and stillness, while the birds sang around or flitted noiseless through the house, until by the sun falling in at my west window, or the noise of some traveller's wagon on the distant highway, I was reminded of the lapse of time. I grew in those seasons like corn in the night, and they were far better than any work of the hands would have been. They were not time subtracted

from my life, but so much over and above my usual allow-
ance. I realized what the Orientals mean by contemplation and
the forsaking of works. For the most part, I minded not how
the hours went. The day advanced as if to light some work of
mine; it was morning, and lo, now it is evening, and nothing
memorable is accomplished. Instead of singing like the birds,
I silently smiled at my incessant good fortune. As the sparrow
had its trill, sitting on the hickory before my door, so had I
my chuckle or suppressed warble which he might hear out of
my nest. . . . This was sheer idleness to my fellow-townsmen,
no doubt; but if the birds and flowers had tried me by their
standard, I should not have been found wanting. A man must
find his occasions in himself, it is true. The natural day is very
calm, and will hardly reprove his indolence. (W 83–84)

"So had I my chuckle." Thoreau was in his late twenties and early
thirties when he wrote *Walden.* Perhaps only a young man can let the sun
shine on him and count on the moon to make him grow; perhaps only
a young woman can be content with the outward indolence and inward
busyness of growth. An older person has usually succumbed to the need for
stuff to do. Emerson merely seems to us older, not wiser, when he complains
of Thoreau that "he had no ambition" and that "instead of engineering
for all America, he was the captain of a huckleberry-party" (SW 427; cf. J
362). No idle hands, no idle hours, no chuckles, the cuckoo clock now a
factory whistle or a school bell or a prison siren—or, nowadays, the entirely
internalized 24/7, which, mathematically considered, yields an irrational
number of bootless repetitions. I myself have become infected with this
24/7, this frenetic time of boundless busyness, and I wish I could become
as lazy as our good Henry.
      My own way of watching the day go by is measured in pine branches.
After breakfast (smoothie, tea, homemade bread baked by a neighbor
in a wood burning oven, and porridge or muesli), I snatch my trusty
Steckenspitzer and head into the woods. (A *Steckenspitzer* is a half-length
machete with a witch's nose; the blade is keen, the steel thick and heavy, the
leather-wound handle sure and good in the heft.) With the *Steckenspitzer,*
you rake the side branches of pine and fir until they are free of needles
and twigs. You toss the bare *Bengel* onto a pile near the path and look up
to see the sun drifting silently from crown to crown, morning to evening,
breakfast to supper. Even though you have neglected to bring a lunch, as
Thoreau would have approved, since lunches are useless, the day will pass

in a moment. Your hands are too busy and your nose is too filled with luscious scents to notice the time. By evening your wrist is feeling the effects of the *Steckenspitzer*'s torque, and the path is dotted with piles of stripped and fragrant branches.

As you head for home—you can drag the piles of branches down to the cabin on a trusty old sled tomorrow when you are fresh—you count the piles the way a writer counts the pages, although with greater satisfaction and more confidence. Once you have sawed the stripped *Tannenbengel* down to the stove's bite size, they will warm you without fail. Pages, eked out with so much scratching of head and pen, are so fleeting in the fire and go up in smoke so fast they can serve only as ignition, whereas the evergreen branches burn and burn, then glow as red coals on into the night, proving that even the night can be auroral.

18

Freaks of nature; or,
lighting fires and mourning the woods

After offering us a chilling account of ice bubbles, Thoreau warms up to his subject in "House-Warming." Like him, but a century and a half after him, I gather the wood that lies on the forest floor, "gleaning after the wood chopper" (W 190). Like Thoreau, I am a scavenger, depriving the woods of a portion of its future humus. After days of such gleaning, however, having gathered enough wood to warm me for the winter, I cannot see a speck of difference in the forest; there seems to be as much fallen wood as ever, as though the woodpile beneath my window were an illusion. Scavengers—such as Thoreau, Marlonbrando, and I—love the forest *and* the woodpile. "Every man looks at his wood-pile with a kind of affection" (W 191). That is too weak a word. One needs a churchgoing sort of word, or a lovemaking sort of word. That is what a woodpile evokes. My own

is a bit harum-scarum, I admit, whereas my neighbors' woodpiles are the very essence of architecture. (An architect friend assures me, however, that genuine architecture is constructed from the scraps and debris of the design studio, not from the polished models, and to that extent my ragamuffin woodpile is authentic architecture—or, as I like to call it, *arche-ticture*.) The forester's woodpile boasts the façade of the Bank of England, with every log locked in place, symmetrical and massively secure. Mine is shanty Irish. Yet it stays dry even on a rainy night like this, and, when I feed a piece to my stove, it glows with gratitude.

Thoreau says he starts his fires with dry leaves and "green hickory finely split" (ibid.). I start mine with old manuscripts—something of my own—and slivers of dry pine. Chopping those pine starters is one of life's greatest pleasures: the piece of wood shivers from top to bottom; makes a lovely cracking sound; shows smooth, clean, blond flanks; and is deliciously fragrant. Thoreau is a friend of green wood in general, "hard green wood just cut" (W 192), whereas I prefer seasoned wood and believe my chimney does too. Regardless of our divergent preferences, however, the two of us are friends of the forest. Thoreau is in fact more than a friend of wood and woods; he is an authentic aficionado. Whereas his descriptions of food are meager, his words relating to wood are succulent: "A few pieces of fat pine were a great treasure. It is interesting to remember how much of this food for fire is still concealed in the bowels of the earth" (ibid.). He means the roots of felled or fallen trees, though how he ever extracted or hacked away at these root systems is beyond my comprehension—he admits that his axe grew dull.

About that axe. Thoreau says, near the outset of his book, "I borrowed an axe and went down to the woods by Walden Pond" (W 29). He brags that he returned the axe sharper than he received it, but the return must have been difficult. For it turns out that three different people lent him that prolific axe. The editor of the Variorum edition of *Walden* tells us that folks got in line to lend him that axe: Amos Bronson Alcott, a neighbor, handed over the Bunyanesque tool, "and with this he [Thoreau] built the temple of a grand primeval man" (W 266n. 109); an early commentator counters that the axe came from Emerson, from whom Thoreau borrowed everything else; whereas, finally, Ellery Channing, "in his own copy of *Walden*, has a note claiming the axe as his" (ibid.). Three axes to grind? I'll know that I have made it as an author when three neighbors of mine dispute the loan of my first Bic, even if the Bic has in the meantime become a Waterman, the Waterman a Pelican, and the Pelican a Mac. But let's drop the three axes—carefully, off to the side—and get back to the woods.

39

Thoreau cites an English authority who laments the impact of trespassers on the flora and fauna of the forest. Like Thoreau, I am a trespasser, though not the worst of these, I hope. Last week, I politely reprimanded a city couple who were letting their dog run free in the woods to frighten the deer. (City dogs never catch up with the deer, but the does often miscarry as a result of the chase.) The woman snapped back at me that her dog was from the Animal Rescue League and that she above all persons loved animals. Ah, yes, people and their pets, people and their doggone logic.

Henry David says that when any part of the forest burns he grieves, and I believe him. Like Wordsworth, he hugs trees, and not merely to make sure they are there. In fact, Thoreau is never more tender than when he accompanies a felled tree to its final resting place, and this seems right to me. "I grieved with a grief that lasted longer and was more inconsolable than that of the proprietors; nay, I grieved when it was cut down by the proprietors themselves" (W 190). What a shift has occurred in our own day, when a secretary of the interior sells off virgin national forest to make newsprint for gossip rags (*newsprint* is a misnomer) or to grant the frackers free reign. It is not as though we have lost our sense of the sacred. That, in God's own country, we nonindigenous folk never had. We have lost our sense of the absurd.

Thoreau dreams of a mythic time when trees were holy. "I would that our farmers when they cut down a forest felt some of that awe which the old Romans did when they came to thin, or let in the light to, a consecrated grove (*lucum conlucare*), that is, would believe it is sacred to some god. The Roman made an expiatory offering, and prayed, Whatever god or goddess thou art to whom this grove is sacred, be propitious to me, my family, and children, &" (ibid.).

Thoreau's allusion reminds me of one of my favorite phrases, *lucus a non lucendo*, which is a pun on *lux* and *lucus*, a pun that contains entire philosophies: "A grove where no light penetrates." That is what critics have often said about my own books of philosophy, and they are no doubt correct. I was always reluctant to cut down or chop to size the trees on which I was commenting. It is a shame that our dictionaries, in the Foreign Words and Phrases section, no longer list the *lucus a non lucendo*. They skip over the sacred grove and go from *locum tenens* (inhabitant) to *lusus naturae* (freak of nature). Nowadays, only a freak would regard the forest grove as something sacred, whereas the inhabitants—or the grove's title holders and the venal politicians they install—just want to sell it off for profit.

H.D. in bed

He writes little about it—about that third of our lives we spend in bed—except in the chapter on "Economy." There he is compelled to broach the subject, for the bed has to do with warmth and hence with vital heat. Food is the fuel for such heat, and firewood also helps prepare and sustain it in more than one way. Clothing and shelter are all about husbanding the heat provided by food and firewood, preserving it above all when we go to bed. Our beds are our nightclothes, says Thoreau, pajamas starched into headboard and steeled into bedstead. We rob "the nests and breasts of birds," he continues, to insulate "this shelter within a shelter, as the mole has its bed of grass and leaves at the end of its burrow!" (W 9). That's about it, as far as "H.D. in bed" is concerned.

Except for a warning later in the book about "sleeping sensually." Sleeping sensually? Alone in a cabin at Walden Pond? I wonder what this admonition means. For I have not yet been able to sleep intellectually, except during convocation and commencement exercises at the university. No, when I am in bed, I close my eyes and dim down my ears, make my comfort movements in the fluff and folds of the featherbed (that little bit of heaven! of the nests and breasts of birds!) and imitate altogether sensually the sleep I wish to come. If she is not there, my dear one, I wish her there. I dwell on her in ways that Thoreau would doubtless condemn. If luck is with me, she puts her head on my shoulder, and we laugh and talk in ways he would surely also condemn. We may plunder the nests and breasts of birds for our bed, but both Marion and Leopold Bloom attest to the infinite superiority of human calefaction over every other sort. If I am alone in the cabin, it is seldom by choice. My loyal featherbed tries to compensate. It is made from the down of an angel's wing, the wing, says a friend of mine, you wrap around the ones you love when they are far away. Thoreau would be the first to admit that vital or genial heat has to do with the imagination but the last to admit that the imagination helps us sleep sensually. One has to fear that H.D.'s imagination was no good in bed.

H.D. in bed? Henry Dolittle, one might say, making a bad literary pun—and an uncharitable one to boot. Let charity cover a multitude instead, cover them like a featherbed, an angel's wing. As for me, let the cabin be hospitable to, if not promiscuous with, sensual sleep.

Maudlin and bathetic

It was a terrible day when, still in high school but already studying M.H. Abrams' *Glossary of Literary Terms*, I read the article on bathos. I thought at first the word meant "pathos" and was merely oddly spelled. But no— *bathos*: from the Greek word for depths, βαθύς, especially the deep sea, the briny blue, meaning in rhetoric and literature the plunge from dizzying heights and profoundly felt depths (*de profundis*) to mere sentimentality and heart-on-sleeve superficiality. "The bathetic of our women novelists," growls Curmudgeon the Critic in the *Oxford English Dictionary*, "verbose when they should have been concise, bathetic when they wanted to be pathetic." By *pathetic*, he means of course reflecting deeply felt emotion. He rages about our little women, "declining . . . to the very bathos of insipidity." And yet Curmudgeon the Critic has a devastating effect on me whenever I write about my childhood experiences or about my family, especially my mother and father, or even about my dream life. How do you write about your family or your lovers without plunging into bathos? Can even our little men avoid that?

Bathos is exactly what happened years ago when I tried to evoke, through the self-hypnosis of writing, my earliest memories: I wrapped myself in the winding cloth of an alien and affected style to protect myself from the feelings that overwhelmed me, when all I wanted to elicit were those very feelings—floating on my back like Blake's Urizen in the matricial sea of memory. Instead, I ironized, I wrote on stilts, I pulled every trick and trope I had learned from Abrams to conceal my knowledge of self—the knowledge of my inevitable and inexpugnable bathos, my entirely superficial depth that was still far too deep for me. I was in way over my head. What was I in terror of? The answer is clear. Just listen to the language of Curmudgeon the Critic: our women . . . impotent . . . verbose . . . insipidity. What's a boy to do when confronted with abyssal depths of feeling but gird up his loins and run like a milksop?

Maudlin, in its sweetest possible sense, means a penitent who resembles Mary Magdalene. That is, phrased somewhat less sweetly, what used to be called a "floozy" posing as a tearful Meryl Streep. "To play a poor lamenting Mawdlines part," purrs our captious Curmudgeon.

Just now Frédéric Chopin's eighth nocturne—opus 27, no. 2—began to play, the nocturne that always stops me in my tracks. Shall I write about what it does to my heart? Are we ready for that—in an aphorism on the maudlin and bathetic? Are we steeled against the plunge? No feeling of the heart and only the rarest piece of music can be described without the maudlin and the bathetic. Ambitious young musicologists therefore despise Chopin as though he were Hugh Grant.

Maudlin: "Alluding to pictures in which the Magdalene was represented weeping," hence tearful, lachrymose. "Like Heraclitus the Maudlin Philosopher . . . characterized by tearful sentimentality, mawkishly emotional, weakly sentimental." (That is a Heraclitus I have never encountered, to be sure.) Listen again to the language, with lots of adverbs there to help where no help is needed: *mawkishly* emotional, *weakly* sentimental, as though sentiment and emotion required mawkish modifiers. "Used to designate that stage of drunkenness which is characterized by the shedding of tears and effusive displays of affection." Mawkishly effusive displays of weakly impotent emotion and insipidly bathetic sentimentality, weeping what are called "the Tears of the Tankard." We might call it "a tear and a chaser." The liquidity of both orality and urogenitality reduced to their most ignominious and humiliating form: "Some maudlayne dronke, mourning loudly and hye."

To repeat, that was not Abrams but the *Oxford English Dictionary*, with centuries of curmudgeonly critical clout behind it, ready to come down on the head of any fellow with fellow feeling. What does *mawkish* mean, anyway? It sounds like the seedcake that Marion tongues into Poldy's mouth with kisses up there on Howth Head. So, the question seems to be: How does writing get to the seedcake we all hunger for while spurning the seedy and eschewing the needy? How to avoid bathos, circumvent the maudlin? By writing transcendentally, perhaps? That's the usual way to guarantee depth of thought and flatness of emotion. Yet I would trade all the transcendentals for a wink from a too liquid eye. (She needn't be inebriated.) So, why am I afraid to write what I believe and feel?

Add your dreams, and not just the sexy ones!

That is what a wise friend counsels me concerning these "conversations." Perhaps she has read Emerson's *Journals*: "I owe real knowledge and even alarming hints to dreams. . . . For the soul in dreams has a subtle synthetic power which it will not exert under the sharp eyes of the day" (J 403). Add my dreams? Without bathos? Perhaps I could tell them to Marlonbrando?

Tell Marlonbrando your dreams, honey, and everything will be all right

Think of him playing the role of the psychiatrist—obese and brooding and
unutterably wise—who counsels the hero of *Don Juan Demarco*. That can't
be bad: it puts you in Johnny Depp's position, as the swashbuckling ladies'
man, the youthful Don Giovanni himself. Try to see the psychiatrist the way
Faye Dunaway sees him. Spill your unconscious beans into the basket of his
distracted mumbles; try to realize that it isn't Don Corleone you're talking
to anymore; this isn't going to kill you. Open that tiny green notebook
you keep at your bedside, the one with *Traumbuch* (dream book) scrawled
across its first page. Skip the drear stuff, and let the sexy ones go; clean up
the scatology a touch and tell the people (no, tell Marlonbrando) about
your "task dreams." That's what you call them, isn't it, task dreams? You are
wary. You are suspicious about all this. Marlonbrando crouches on the sill,
indifferent to your suspicions, haunted by his own. You are the first to speak.

—I don't see your license hanging on the wall.

—License? I don't have a license. Dogs have licenses.

—I mean your license to practice psychotherapy.

—I have poetic license. That allows me to drive every sort of literary
vehicle over the roughest terrain.

—Will you have the slightest inkling of what I am saying? Do cats
have dreams?

Marlonbrando's eyes glaze over, whether out of defensiveness or
contempt I cannot say.

—It's your one-hundred-and-three dollars per forty-five minutes. Start
talking.

The penmanship of the *Traumbuch* is a disgrace, I admit. My dream
book contains inchoate, incoherent scribblings jotted down in the middle
of the night. My intention is always to expand on the key words contained
in this tiny notebook, writing out the full account of the dream in my
journal the following morning. Usually the mornings have their way with
me, however, and I forget all about those cryptic ciphers of the night; the

Traumbuch rests on my nightstand, waiting patiently for the next installment of illegible scratchings. Yet on occasion I do manage to spin out a dream or two in my journal. For one January 17, for example, I find in my dream book the notation, "The War of the Roses," and the following account in my journal: "Rose rustlers arrive at the hacienda, gun down grandma on the doorstep, shoot and kill all the farm hands, toss a grenade at the writhing corpses—and walk off with dozens of American Beauties wrapped in cellophane." In order that the dream be taken seriously, I note that the mood of the dream—so ridiculous in the recounting—is "serious and foreboding." Serious and foreboding, as with all my task dreams. My journal also records the following dream dreamt three nights prior to "The War of the Roses":

> I am kneeling at the rail of a choir loft beside my mother. Some fantastical liturgy is going on down below, all very Italianate. We then understand that we are listening to a reading of the latest Papal Bull. It appears in gigantic Greek letters on a movie screen: they are in an ancient script, the letters yellowed with age. I half-recognize some of the words, such as
>
> θεολογικῶν,
>
> referring to matters of theological import. Yet most of it is incomprehensible to us. Mother and I begin to be bored.

At this point in my recounting of the dream, I cannot suppress the mirth that bubbles up in me. I cry out to Marlonbrando.

—One might well say that this was *all* Papal bull!

—No witty intrusions, retorts Marlonbrando. Just tell us the dream.

—I was only trying to spice it up a bit.

—You were calling on cleverness to conceal something you are afraid to acknowledge in the dream.

—Bull!

—Precisely. What is it you are afraid of?

—My mother's look.

—Why? Is she angry with you?

—No, not angry. Not at all . . .

Marlonbrando tells me to continue reading from my journal, cautioning me once again about intrusions, insertions, evasions, stilts, bathos. I read:

. . . begin to be bored. We sit back on our haunches. Mother looks at me—silently, because we are still in church. She is old and wrinkled, but her eyes are still bright and clear. She looks at me with intense love and approval, with a blessing beyond mere acceptance. (I received these looks in real life, accompanied with an "Oh, David!" perhaps when I handed her a new book or did some other praiseworthy thing, or maybe when I came to see her in the hospital, having traveled from the cabin back to the States in order to do so.) It is the look Hölderlin craved from his own mother when he wrote to her, "Accept me as I am." A loving look, then, but perhaps *too* loving; there is something of disapproval in it; no, even worse, something of *forgiveness*. She is forgiving me for something I have done, but I cannot live up to her forgiveness. The look makes me want to say something, but I am worried about the indiscretion or inappropriateness of it, and I hold back for a moment. Finally, I blurt it out: "I just want you to live for a long time, and to be well!" Her response is to let me know, not through words but by means of that look, that she is already dead. I awake engaged in the effort to calculate the years it has been since she died.

—Tell us about this calculation of the years. How long has your mother been dead?

—I don't know. I forget.

—You forget?

—I always forget. I have to work it out each time. Not the day, which I'm clear about, April 18, but the year. I always have to perform some sort of subtraction or other more abstruse arithmetic procedure. When I'm still not sure, I ask my oldest sister. She tells me: 1996.

—Most boys are able to remember the year of their mother's death. Maybe that's why she has to forgive you?

—I don't want to talk about it.

—Good. We are making progress. Tell me about that look of hers.

—She looks at me with infinite love and patience and forgiveness.

—And that look makes you feel more guilty than ever?

—Exactly!

Marlonbrando toys with his ballpoint, then fixes me with a stare.

—Infinite love, you say? Is your mother looking at you with . . . desire?

—What do you mean, desire? Don't be silly, she's my mother.

47

Marlonbrando suppresses a smile. Analysts are so smug.

—Well, then. Tell us about your father's death.

—1978.

—You have no trouble remembering that one. Go on.

—There are no dreams of his death recorded in the *Traumbuch*. I had dreams of him earlier on, spectacular ones. Later on, there is only one strange dream about him after his death—it's about my dad giving me a Bloomberry bush.

—Blueberry?

—Bloomberry. As though alluding to Woolf. Or echoing Joyce, more likely.

Marlonbrando writes down the names with difficulty.

—Go on.

This dream too was recorded on the following morning, so that once again I can read to the feral analyst the elaborated version from my journal:

The dream begins with my walking alongside the old cement wall that supported our front lawn and separated it from the driveway. (This is at the home where I lived from ages three to twenty.) Whereas the wall used to be cracked and shabby, it is now freshly adobed, finished in a seamless silvery concrete. In fact, farther down the way, the wall rises to become the high curved wall of the house itself—an adobe fortress, monumental, with tiny windows (by Le Corbusier, evidently) and a grand porch. No more stucco or asphalt shingle! It is wonderful in my dream to follow the sweep of that sinuous wall up to the brilliant sky!

My dad is in the garage, squatting on the floor, putzing around with assorted nuts and bolts. *Putzing* was one of his favorite words.

—What are you doing? I ask him.

—Oh, putzing around.

Putzing, with a short *u*: *pútt-sing*. Perhaps the adobe concrete is *Putz*, the German word for the outside plaster of a house. *Putz* is also one of the Yiddish words for the penis, although there are no explicit *putzes* in my dream. In any case, my dad is putzing around with nuts and bolts on the floor of the dilapidated garage—where he used to repair, endlessly and futilely, the succession of gas-powered lawn mowers that my older brother had to push all around the yard for hours, mowing my Dad's golf-course lawn. I often dream about that vast yard.

My dad looks young and sprightly, squatting on the floor there, but I know that he is old and a widower. (In my dream, mother is as long dead to my dad as he was to her in real life.) We take a walk through the back yard, once a paradise of rose trellises, flower and vegetable beds, and green lawn. Now motor graders have leveled the hills and stripped away the lawn. Junked cars are littered about everywhere. I am shocked. My dad is now walking well ahead of me, so I have to shout.

—Dad, what happened?

—Aw, nobody cares anymore, he grumbles.

He now says something in that arch, mincing voice he used whenever he was being sarcastic, to cover up his embarrassment or hurt—a very common gesture with him.

—People say I have a *temper*, that I am tempera*mental*, and that I always speak first and think only later!

He walks farther and farther ahead, into the encroaching city. I can no longer hear what he is saying. We walk past ugly store-front buildings in a typical city neighborhood; the idyll has been left behind. My dad, in spite of his stride, seems old and senile. He has a bad heart. I struggle to catch up with him so that I can hear what he is saying.

When I do catch up, he is grimacing with pain. I urge him to sit down at a sidewalk cafe we happen to be passing.

—When do you have to go? he asks me.

—Tomorrow, I reply.

He is silent but I can see that he is dispirited. In that mincing voice of his, he begins to say sarcastic things to a woman sitting next to us.

—I'll bet you didn't know it back then when he gave you those *steel* things, did you? he says snidely, pointing at some gaudy jewelry she is wearing. She pretends not to hear him. The two of us are looking more and more like Alfred and Chip of Jonathan Franzen's *The Corrections*.

Suddenly, the cafe is a shoe store, and a young man is trying to squeeze a black loafer past my dad's bunions. My dad yelps in pain; the lad smiles in embarrassment. I determine to get my father back home. He is disconsolate, and so I tell him I'll stay a couple days longer.

—Of course I'll stay.

He doesn't show it directly, but he is elated by this news. Clearly, I am Chip. As we reenter the ruined idyll—ruined, but there is that graceful adobe wall again, rising to the sky—he pauses before a large espaliered bush. It is like a vast inverted fan, a brilliant green fern with large bright green berries. I am entranced. I put my face right into it.

—What is it? I ask.

—Bloomberry, he replies.

Not blueberry. Bloomberry. He clips a sprig of Bloomberry, carries it into the house, and puts it into a vase—in my honor, in honor of my staying. The beautiful green fern exudes a mood of peace and harmony. It is a restoration of home. Yet the mood of the dream is for the most part troubled: I have to chase after him, care for him. The only two objects that relieve the sense of anxiety and helplessness are the high adobe wall and the beautiful spade of Bloomberry.

I can see that Marlonbrando is affected by this dream. He blinks slowly, does not break the silence. Slowly he opens wide his golden eyes. His gaze transfixes me.

—Silently over the Place of the Skull open God's golden eyes, murmurs Marlonbrando.

Neighbors, Part Two: Herr S.W.

He is the neighbor I most enjoy talking to, although each conversation takes a lot of time. His words—always the right ones, approved by the critical mind of the reflective narrator—come slowly and softly up from the diaphragm and set the velvet vocal chords to vibrating. His pale blue eyes open wide at the punchline of each story he tells. This man is very smart, and he is a master of timing, a first-rate raconteur. He makes even a pleonasm sound like a grand synthesis. When he raises his wine glass in a toast, what comes out of his mouth is sheer tautology and pure gold.

—*E bis Guets 's e bis Guets.* (A little something good is a little something good.)

The wine always tastes better after this pleonastic benediction and ritual redundancy. Furthermore, the toastmaster and raconteur always has his eye fixed on the ironies and calamities of the modern world, even when he is mowing the hay with a scythe in front of his house.

—I was looking at an advertisement for the national railway in the newspaper today. It said, "Faster! Farther! No limit!" And I remembered a pamphlet the *Luftwaffe* [the German Air Force] distributed to us just before the outbreak of the war. On the cover it said, "Faster! Farther! No limit!"

He was leaning on his scythe as he told me this cautionary tale. When he finished, and he was not smiling, his pale, wide-open eyes held me, and then, blinking, released me; he stood up straight and continued with his steady sway, swing, and stroke, making the grass go *hush! hush! hush!*

24

The darkness of the woods

Thoreau writes about making his way home through the woods at night, and his description is perfect: "It is darker in the woods, even in common nights, than most suppose. I frequently had to look up at the opening between the trees above the path in order to learn my route" (W 129). It is strange to have to make one's way by looking up, not down, and Thoreau could have made transcendentalist capital out of that, as he does out of almost everything. He always likes to steer by the most distant glinty star. Yet the milky way through the woods is in fact more literal than literary, and I often find myself craning my neck to get a better feel for my path. Of course, if there is no moon, or if the fog is too thick, and if a log or a large stone has fallen or rolled across the path, not even heaven can help. I then need the advanced technology of the flashlight, which operates on that sometime thing called a battery. The greatest pleasure afforded by the flashlight, however, even when the batteries are fresh, is when you click it off, and, your eyes adjusting, though never fast enough, you ply the night unaided. Over the years, I've fallen only once in these woods, and that was when a car's high beams behind me (on a path where no car should have been) confused me with light. Though it is never reassuring, the dark is safer.

Monarchs in December

I was out at the woodshed gathering an armful of nourishment for a starving fire when I heard a strange brushing noise, subdued, but repeated several times and almost rhythmic in its insistence. I looked down to a tarp near the ground and saw a young monarch butterfly opening and shutting its brilliant wings—reddish-orange freckles among black and white spots, with a vast Elizabeth Taylor eye at each tip. The temperature was well below freezing; an icing of hoarfrost covered the morning meadow. A newly crowned monarch in December? A king hatched in winter? Clearly, nature had miscalculated. I hoped my leather gloves would not damage the delicate wings.

I brought it inside and fed it diluted honey from a teaspoon. The nectar and the warmth revived the monarch: he or she—for a monarch may be a queen—fluttered violently against the windowpane that faces south. I hesitated. Should I grant royalty its freedom? Or did freedom mean certain death? I decided to keep the window closed and to make a pet of royalty. I did not see it again for four days. Some pet! Yet its ghost haunted the cabin, *Remember me!* even if I could not locate the body, or the two bodies, of the king. Nature did seem to have miscalculated—but the miscalculation lay with the well-meaning human, not with the monarch.

Four days after having rescued it, as I was enjoying cookies and muscat wine with a friend, the monarch fluttered down onto a manuscript page, then flew against the windowpane. The day was not nearly so cold. I opened the window and watched the monarch fly into the open arms of Douglas the Fir.

Today, Christmas morning, four days after the release of the monarch, I was in the kitchen washing the dishes when I heard once again the flutter of wing against windowpane. I hurried into the stube and saw another monarch desperate for the freedom of the outside world. I couldn't open the window this time because my superfluous Christmas tree was blocking it. So I trapped it gently in a plastic sack and carried it to the front door of the cabin. I released the monarch and once again watched it fly to freedom and certain death.

Will I find yet another spirit of kings and queens haunting the cabin come New Year's? Are they cocooning without *and* within the cabin? Am I the breeding ground of the royals? Or is the cabin a graveyard of original spiritual manifestations? Certain death, did I say? Is death ever uncertain?

The limits of description

"Unsettling as a warm December." That is a sentence I wrote once while on a bus wending its way through the Pyrenees from Seu d'Urgel to Barcelona. I no longer remember the occasion, but clearly I was worried about something. Once again December, now in its final days, is too warm. Everyone in the valley is anxious for winter to arrive. The forester complains about the number of flies in the stall.

—It's like July in there. Shameless!

On my way back home from the forester's, walking the stretch of path that leads through the woods of the Hörnli beyond Barley Stalk Hill, I suddenly became aware that it was soon going to snow. How did I know this? *Know* is too strong a word, of course, but it is the very word that falls. I *knew* of impending snow. Every person born and bred in the north is certain about how we know: it has to do with a certain unmistakable quality of light. How to describe it?

In heraldry, one would say something like "pines on a field of argent resplendent." It is no doubt that peculiar argentine quality of the light—the silvery light that betrays snow—that needs to be described. The sky is leaden, and all the objects that appear against its backdrop are gray-on-gray. Yet now gray is no longer entirely gray. Gray is now illuminated from within, as though by a phosphorescent, incandescent silvery sprite. Perhaps the quality of light, the silvery luminescence, is influenced by the chill in the wind? It is not cold enough yet to snow—the superficies of my skin tells me that—but it is cold enough to trouble the rain, to alter the droplets in a way that beggars description. Perhaps the chill in the wind exudes a certain odor? For it begins to *smell* like snow. Yet what is the fragrance of future snow? Perhaps the sense of smell is reinforced by another sense, the sense of a premonitory dream or intimation, a kind of augury, a faculty of meteorological metaphysics. Who knows? But it is going to snow very soon.

27

The limits of knowledge

Days have passed and still it hasn't snowed. "Unsettling as a warm December."

Black and white

After a night of snowfall, the day lights up painfully slowly, without a trace of sun and without a hint of color. Schauinsland Mountain glowers darker gray under a slate gray sky, its larches, pines, and firs no longer ever green but black. The Black Forest. The pasture in front of the cabin is untracked, untrammeled. The trees close by, mostly birches, are penciled black lines straining under painted white burdens. Windstill. All the colors have bled from these pallid shades of gray, and yet the result is nothing stark: the edges of all things are muted by snowy overhangs, as pasture melds into mountain, mountain into sky. The windows of the cabin serve as picture frames in an old sketchbook or photo album of the family—of my parents' families—except that there are only two photographs here, one hanging on the east wall, the other on the south. Windows as still lifes. Windstill still lifes. Until a magpie flits by, itself black and white, on the diagonal.

29

Fool's spring

As there is fool's gold, so there is fool's spring. Whether in January or March there will be days—O the blessings of worldwide industry and global warming!—when the sun shines so unseasonably warm and the wind is so unseasonably still that one can don a light jacket and sit and contemplate the cabin from the outside. Douglas the Fir perfumes the crisp air, the birds strike up a song, and all the world conspires to say,

—Tra-la! Spring time is rilly-dilly-ding time, and the hammer of winter will never fall again!

We know the lyric is a lie, but both our mind and our senses are seduced. It is carnival season anyway, so put on your Fool's cap and scribble on foolscap that winter storms are a thing of the past, a mere meteorological misunderstanding, an anomaly, a chimera! It's rilly-dilly-ding time!

Your eye glances up to the chimney. You weren't so bamboozled that you neglected to light a fire against the advancing evening chill. You see the smoke drifting south and west toward the setting sun, which means that the north wind, Boreas, is blowing. That explains the brilliant blue sky, since precipitation comes out of the south and west. Boreas wears velvet gloves today. And in his gloved hand, you have to fear, the hammer.

A reflection on consumer society; or, a Romantic has his uses

"Now it is time for gods to emerge from things with which we dwell." Rainer Maria Rilke is thinking here of an empty water pitcher or wine jug, an item of stoneware that has been in the house as long as anyone can remember. Nowadays the pitcher is always empty, because water comes in plastic bottles and wine in throwaway glass bottles. We don't wait for the pitcher to be refilled; we go out and buy a prepackaged replacement. The difference between enjoying and consuming is in the packaging. Enjoyment is never packaged, whereas consuming is all in the packaging, all in the cardboard cellophane plastic aluminum foil and glass. It is the difference between bread and wine and Pop Tarts and Gatorade. Throwaway goods, throwaway gods, for throwaway folk.

One might counter that modern technologized life puts us in closer touch with many things—for example, with food not on the kitchen table but on the food channel, or at best the gutta-percha feel of exotic oyster mushrooms trucked in from Pennsylvania or Poland. For some bizarre reason, here at the cabin I think of my modern technologized life in connection with the laundry.

I used to do my laundry by hand in two big plastic tubs. Among the grand pleasures of life was the transmutation of clammy clothing to sparkling colors and lambent whites on the line, to see what soap and sun and time can do when left alone. (Even Pallas Athena did the laundry, Homer tells us.) It is possible to feel a tinge of sadness on a sunny day when there is insufficient laundry to warrant a wash. One goes looking for it, digging up gamy dish towels and stained placemats and redolent rags to constitute a quorum. What else are warm summer nights made for but kissing a friend on the nape of the neck—knowing that, barring rain, the socks will be dry by morning, smelling of Douglas the Fir and rampant oxygen?

I hear the housewife laughing at me, and the houseman too, along with the single gal or guy who hates that mountain of wash. You are right, of course. I've been spoiled for so long that these pleasures of the kitchen and the laundry room are still unspoiled for me. What can I say? Bring me your socks and things—some of you at least. Bring me, some of you at least, your wispy napes of neck. A Romantic has his uses.

Oh, and the modern tools! I bought an expensive chef's knife in the big city—actually a friend bought it for me as a present. I keep it in the tray with the other utensils of the cabin kitchen, but in a plastic sheath so the edge won't nick. I wish I had a leather sheath for it, it is so noble a tool. I use this knife only on special occasions—when an eggplant needs cutting lengthwise into very thin slices so that it can be baked with mozzarella and basil leaf and plum tomatoes or when a honeydew melon needs to be halved and quartered and cut into eighths to rendezvous with prosciutto. The heft of the knife is so satisfying, so balanced; it graces the hand that wields it. And the edge is like a true, original thought, which cuts through everything. A dull knife is a terrible sin, and I'm always surprised how many otherwise decent people will commit it. Scores of sinners of my acquaintance, when they invite me to their homes, ask me to bring my whetstone with me so I can sharpen all their knives. Sinners don't even own a whetstone, just a millstone around their napes. Or they have—hiding somewhere in a junk drawer—a hickeymajigger that looks like a can opener but in reality is an insult to a Confessor and Healer of Knives like me. I enter their kitchen as a Pontiff in ritual drag and I expiate the dullness of their knives and their lives, knowing full well that they will need me again, the backsliders.

Well, now, what a silly boy I am, with my napes and socks and whetstones! What things a Romantic won't take pride in! Or *will* take pride in!

Postscript. Some years ago, the Romantic bought himself a washing machine, a small toploader. The end of Romance? I don't know. It has no window, my machine, but often when it is sucking water and spinning like a dancer and spewing suds I sit on the edge of the bathtub and gape at it as though it were a television.

The deserving poor

Henry's patronizing of the poor would not be worth noting if it weren't such a one hundred percent US-American attitude, as ubiquitous today as it was in his time. For Henry, of course, it is the Irish who are the deserving poor. His accounts of them in *Walden* range from pitying condescension to pitiless exploitation, so much so that the editor of the Variorum *Walden* feels constrained to insert a note explaining that in "real life" Thoreau was kinder to the Irish than anyone else was. Well, then, heaven help the Irish! Perhaps it is simply that the New Englander of the 1840s, in his or her attitude toward the Irish, was still like the Old Englanders from Cromwell onward: contempt spiced with violence. The Irish whom Thoreau meets are either shantytown laborers working on the railroads or bogtrotters draining swamps. They ought to be discussed in his chapter called "Brute Neighbors," except that the Irish haven't the dignity and grace of animals.

Thoreau seeks shelter under the shabby roof of the Irishman John Field (not the composer) at Baker Farm. Poor John Field! He hires himself out too cheaply, toils endlessly, and doesn't know how to fish. He and his family are bound to stay right where they are—in deserved destitution. Thoreau writes: "With his horizon all his own, yet he a poor man, born to be poor, with his inherited Irish poverty or poor life, his Adam's grandmother and boggy ways, not to rise in this world, he nor his posterity, till their wading webbed bog-trotting feet get *talaria* to their heals" (W 159). Now, *talaria* are the wings attached to Hermes' heels (or, for you florists out there, to Mercury's sandals), so that Thoreau seems to be saying that all the Irish need to become truly human is to be transformed into gods. Perhaps he merely intends to hurry the Irish on their way to heaven.

John Field is not the first Irishman who offers Thoreau shelter. In "Economy," Thoreau tells us that he bought the boards for his cabin from James Collins, another shantytown Irishman. "James Collins' shanty was considered an uncommonly fine one," writes Thoreau (W 31). Nothing but the best for Henry. Thoreau makes Collins an offer he cannot refuse, and Collins does not refuse. "I had to pay four dollars and twenty-five cents tonight, he to vacate at five tomorrow morning, . . . I to take possession at six" (ibid.). The early bird catches the bogtrotting worm. "At six I passed him and his family on the road. One large bundle held their all,—bed, coffee-mill, looking-glass, hens,—all but the cat, she took to the woods and became a wild cat, and, as I learned afterward, trod in a trap set for woodchucks, and so became a dead cat at last" (ibid.). As far as Thoreau is concerned, although there is no need to mention this passage to Marlonbrando, the dead cat indicates the way ahead for the Collins family: Henry bestows wings on the webbed feet of the bogtrotters simply so that they may fly to heaven at last, leaving their earthly goods for Yankees to plunder.

The fundamental US-American ideal is to strike a deal and not be concerned about the other party. Let the buyer or seller beware, a sucker born to Adam's grandmother every minute. And so we think ourselves a generous people and are hated the world over for our amiable callousness, our cheerful and oblivious selfishness, to the point where we are forced to conclude that the deserving poor are simply envious of us.

32

A succession of beautiful days

Goethe says somewhere that a succession of beautiful days is the hardest thing for people to bear. Camus' stranger and Dostoevsky's underground man understand this, but most of us do not—until we live in Germany for a spell, especially in the Black Forest. All that verdure comes from somewhere, after all, and rain is most often the order of the day and of the night in every season. At certain times of the year, rain and fog—which is sideways rain—can last night and day for three weeks and more. It is now late March, and the sun has been shining for a week of days, each day warmer and more sparkling than the last. It is still too cold to write outside at my little blue table, but I am writing outside, bundled in layers and blinded by the light. Playing the fool again. Yet all the while I am wondering whether the barometer is stuck in this optimistic imposture, and where are those rain clouds anyway? I gaze southwest toward the Burgundian Gate and due west to the snow-laden Vosges. Not a cloud in sight. That is because they are hiding somewhere waiting to pounce, waiting for me to drop my guard and slacken my vigilance.

It is like a love affair that is about to collapse. I have heard the creaking timbers and seen the crumbling plaster for months now, yet each time I come together with her the sun shines more blindingly than ever for a succession of days. You would think a lover could simply wait and see, instead of rehearsing over and over again the scenes and the lines of the coming catastrophe, trying to force the issue in order to evade inevitability.

—We'll see, is all she ever says.

Yet is that any reason to be a catastrophist? Whether with or without reasons, I study the Book of Revelations and move like the macabre figures at the end of *Apocalypse Now*, waiting for the impending monsoon and the season of sacrifice. Nothing is harder to bear than a succession of beautiful days.

33

Neighbors, Part Three: Wolfgang

Slow-blinking eyes in an elongated face, lips that never close over his teeth even though he is not grinning, not even smiling. Look at him and you laugh, in spite of what your mother taught you. You laugh even when he is up there tooting earnestly on his piccolo, a measure or two behind the rest of the band. He rarely speaks. Yet he is quite clever: when he is not tooting his piccolo, he is dissecting cadavers. He is a forensic pathologist at the university clinic, which accounts for his deadpan, I suppose.

A small group of us were the last to leave a village wine festival in the wee hours of the morning. Wolfgang's eyes were rolling, his lids drooping.

—Will you be all right tomorrow? a friend asked him with a chuckle.

Wolfgang struggled to regain consciousness, then replied.

—It's not tomorrow I'm worried about. It's today.

34

La pensée du jour

It's like a potage, which is to say, yesterday's leftovers introduced to a blender. That is what a friend calls the aphorisms I am writing here, and she laughs. *La pensée du jour.* She's exactly right, of course, except that my soups are not as palatable as the French chef's. Why write like this? I think it's because I got tired of chasing after thoughts their thinkers deliberately made difficult; tired of scrambling after them, clipping their wings and getting cagey with them; weary of systems developed in twenty or more volumes of tortuous prose. (A professor of mine once wrongly corrected my spelling of this word, writing it as *torturous.* He was a closet philosopher.) No doubt, the aphorism is dead. No one seriously believes the claim that a deft stroke of the pen can capture in a single line what entire volumes say—or, rather, do *not* say, as the naughty Nietzsche has it.

Nevertheless, we today are arguably left with nothing else but *fragmentary* writing. True enough, the fragment, at least in the hands of Maurice Blanchot or Luce Irigaray, remains pithy. That would be the word I hope someone might utter about my own soupy thoughts—pithy. Uttered, I can only hope, by a person who has no lisp.

35

The smartphone in high mountains

We all have seen and heard the go-getter businessman, the thruster, at airport gates. We have all seen and heard him on his smartphone leaving instructions for the incompetents back at the office or preparing the incompetents at his destination for his Coming. He is sometimes jocund and jovial, sometimes impatient and strident, but always dependably loud. We all have also seen and heard the passenger on the bus, subway, or elevated train, letting his or her loved ones in on the essential happenings of the day.

—Hi, I'm on the train. Yeah, it's noisy, so I'll have to shout. Can you hear me? Good. I'm on the train. We just stopped at Addison. How's Uncle Theo's hernia? . . . It's those damn dissolvable stitches, I tell you, they never dissolve, and here it is Thanksgiving and Uncle Theo trussed up like a turkey. . . . Sorry . . . no . . . I know it's not funny. Oops! Belmont! Gotta go, I'll callya from work.

"I'll callya." In Germany, the most popular smartphones, which they call Handies, are fed by *Callya Karten*. These are plastic cards, exorbitantly expensive, on which a secret code number is printed, as though on a lottery ticket. If I rub off the waxy covering and dial that number into the company's computer, it will credit me with a certain number of Euros, and I can callya. Some Germans find the use of these American expressions offensive, while others correctly point out that the final stage of imperialism is capitalism.

"I'll callya." It's a new verb, with no object, taking neither the dative nor the accusative; an intransitive verb, well-nigh in the middle voice, almost reflexive, but not quite reflective. I'll callya, as in I'll take a bath, I'll play the lottery, I'll seeyaround.

There are rules of etiquette governing the use of smartphones in Germany, Switzerland, and Austria, however, and one of these rules is never take your *Callya Karte* smartphone with you on a trek into high mountains. It is quite shocking nevertheless to see how many trekkers violate this well-known rule.

On a ridge high in the Karwendel Range of Austria, where you would think the Handies must be out of range of even the most rarefied satellite waves, you do not have to strain to hear the loudmouth. He is in full trekking gear, sporting all the regalia, everything high end, but here is what he is shouting into his smartphone, presumably to loved ones (difficult to imagine) down in the valley, shouting so loud that the phone seems superfluous.

—It sure is beautiful up here. Yeah, and the weather's perfect. Blue sky. I said *the sky is blue*. Great weather. This is the third valley we've hiked today, one more beautiful than the next, we sure picked the good ones, we were smart.

You hurry on, trying to get out of earshot now that you know the essential matter, namely, how smart both phone and caller are. Yet the mountain is made of stone, and stone echoes.

—Yeah, we're really high. I don't know how high, but we're really high. No, I mean *on the mountain*, ha. Nothing but rock up here. Yeah, and the sky. Bright blue.

You hope that his *Callya Karte* is depleting rapidly and that the silence of the mountains will be restored. Perhaps the ledge on which he is standing, which he mistakes for a phone booth or a soap box, will crumble. Hope springs eternal in high mountains. You remember how Nietzsche always wanted to wander amid icy crags, to be alone with his thoughts, rapt to the silence.

—No trees or nothing. No, we're really high. *On the mountain*, ha. We're about ready to head back though. My feet are killing me—must be the gout again. What? I don't care. Sure, pork steaks, if you want. Thick ones. Just go easy on the sauerkraut, you remember what happened last time, phew!

And that, children, is why there are rules of etiquette governing the use of smartphones in high mountains, and why these rules must be respected.

The new adventures of Pinocchio

Good government is having good people around you, said Ike. So what happens when a hardwood puppet, not ready for the complexities of life, surrounds itself with foxes who serve as puppeteers, foxes and hawks who believe that their self-interest is God's own plan? How do the new adventures of *Pinocchio* turn out? Does the story depend more on the dummy or on the manipulators? Difficult to say. Pinocchio is bound and determined to please old Giapetto at least once in his life, to make a killing on the oil market, or at least a killing, for old Dad. The manipulators, meanwhile, have bigger fish to fry—fish fried in oil, to be sure. The future of the nation is so subject to chance! One doesn't know whether avarice or ignorance will gain the upper hand.

The above paragraph, as the reader may have surmised, was written during the wretched reign of Bush and Cheney. We wanted to believe that the nation could not sink any lower than it did during those years. Yet now we know that the winning hand in the political games of power mongering, racism, xenophobia, vulgarity, venality, violence, and other forms of stupidity has been trumped.

News of the world

Concerning the news of the world Thoreau opines, "To a philosopher all *news*, as it is called, is gossip, and they who edit and read it are old women over their tea" (W 70). Or, one has to add, old men over their bicarbonate of soda. Why the philosophic animus against the news? Heidegger says that every question of the day has to be "de-presentified," on the model of detoxification, where the toxin is everyday superficiality. All the news that's fit to print must have everything quotidian, everything mundane, squeezed out of it. Arch? Snobby? Maybe. Yet what is most interesting about the information age is that most of the information out there is for purposes of distraction and diversion, not information. Why the need to distract? So that the media make money, to be sure. But it is more complicated than that.

The truth is that no one understands what is happening in all the corners of the globe, whether in economics or politics, for it is all both too complex and too well concealed. The only thing we can be sure of is that it will be coming down fire. We need to divert attention from that fact. Back when I was in school, our teachers instructed us to stay abreast of current events so that we could become informed agents of change. Now we know that current events are the sand that the Fox throws in the eyes of the hare.

On the difference between European and American "values"

That was the cover story of a leading news magazine in the United States some years ago, and so I thought I'd better read it. It was during the time when the North Atlantic alliance was strained to the breaking point, the time when French fries, to which Americans owe so much of the national blubber, were being rechristened "freedom fries" to abash the French, who merely laughed. I recall two photographs in the article, one of a prim American couple standing on the steps of their prim Protestant chapel, the other of brazen hussies primping in the show windows of Amsterdam. Yet not only the photojournalism was stellar. The collaborating writers—for it took several of them to write a story with this sort of complexity—indicated that because Europeans are born into their religion they become bored with it and are, by entire populations, losing their faith. Americans, by contrast, because they enjoy the benefits of a free-market economy, have so many ecclesiastical products to choose from that they still manage to believe whatever they do believe from week to week. Not only that. The churches in the United States are interactive: a twist of the joystick and dogma and decor are adjusted to meet the demands of the discerning believer.

The article convinced me, mostly. All it left unexplained was why the American Jesus—across the vast terrain of all those novel features and infinite choices in the American churches—invariably promotes incarcerating, torturing, droning, or at least impoverishing folks all over the world. And why he loves so desperately both the death penalty and the right to life.

Tell Marlonbrando your dreams, honey, and everything will be all right, Part Two

—Can you draw me a picture of this Bloomberry bush?

Marlonbrando pushes a blank sheet of paper across the windowsill. It flutters down onto my writing table. I am, of course, wary.

—This is a trick. It's like the House-Tree-Person test, I complain.

—I don't want the house or the person. Just the tree.

He produces a sketching pencil from his fur-lined vest pocket, sliding it across to me with a single deft motion of his paw—claws extended, as though the pencil were a mouse. I draw, or try to. I'm no Kurt Vonnegut.

—You're right about not being Vonnegut, says Marlonbrando. And even he couldn't draw.

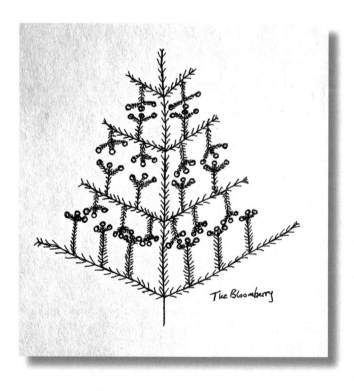

The Bloomberry

—It's not the details of the drawing, it's the feeling that's important—the aura surrounding my father's gift to me.

—The aura? Describe it.

—It is an aura of symmetry. The berries are a translucent, phosphorescent green, the branches a darker hue of green. All of it is alive—evergreen. When he first hands it to me and I gaze at it up close, it seems too perfect to be alive, more a filigreed fan than a fern, more a fern than the Christmas tree it turned out to be in the drawing.

—Is your father connected with Christmas in your memory?

—We were never closer than at Christmas. He was happiest then, or any other time he was able to play with babies and small children. We were all amazed at how silly he could get—he was so stern most of the time.

—Stern?

—He was German.

—Understood. Go on.

—Christmas was a special time for me too when I had children. A glorious time, really. I never believed in the Christ of Xmas, at least once I reached age eleven or twelve, but I always believed in the tree. I still do.

—You and me both. But go on.

—A friend of mine, a philosopher, a really good one, reminded me of his favorite experience of wonder, which is where they say philosophy starts. We were celebrating Christmas Eve together when my son was not yet two. We had real candles on the tree.

—Real candles? As opposed to?

—In America, they wrap strings of electric lights around the tree, lights in the shape of candle flames.

—Sounds dangerous. They could short circuit and cause a fire.

—Agreed. May I go on?

Marlonbrando scowls.

—My son struggled to his feet, entranced by the flame of the candle closest to him. We let him get pretty close. He uttered an exclamatory *O-oooh!*—inadvertently snuffing out the candle. He trembled with excitement. His knees buckled and he went down on his bum. We relit the candle. He got to his feet and *O-oooh'd* it out again. We spent half the night repeating the exercise, to his endless delight, and ours.

—What has this got to do with your father?

—I don't know. But he must have had experiences like that with us kids. All I remember is that Christmas was my favorite time of the year with him, the only time we played . . .

—Tell me about the symmetry, the aura of symmetry about the Bloomberry bush.

—It may have to do with a story about my crazy Uncle Bill. Do you want to hear it?

—Sure . . . You bet . . .

Marlonbrando, savoring the passing time, bends to scrutinize his wristwatch, which keeps on ticking as it takes a licking.

—Forty-five minutes, he purrs. You'll owe me for overtime.

On the degeneration of poetry to chemistry

In his chapter called "House-Warming," Thoreau tells how during his second year in the cabin at Walden Pond he prepared his meals no longer at the open hearth but on a cooking stove, where the fire was no longer visible. He comments: "Cooking was then, for the most part, no longer a poetic, but merely a chemic process" (W 193). In "my" cabin, poetry has deteriorated by yet another degree: at least during the winter months, I cook on two electric plates and in an electric convection oven, where the heating is chillier yet. The house is warmed by fragrant pine and fir, but the cooking remains drab and odorless. In a farmhouse down in the village, many years ago now, I also *cooked* with wood. I learned what every cook from Peking to Paris knows: a wood fire lends savors to a meal that otherwise remain in hiding, not by smoking the food, because that does not happen unless you make a bad fire with bad wood, but by some less obvious process—clearly, a poetic process. Part of the magic is that you use the entire surface of the stove, not merely the "plates," sliding your pots and pans here and there when they call for more or less heat. It is a kind of minuet of pots or a puppet play of pans. And a wood fire produces hot, not chilly, heat. It caresses the food, and its kiss is ardent, its embrace an embrazure.

By way of compensation or restitution, to this day I leave the fire door of the stove that heats my house open for fifteen minutes or so after building my morning fire, partly to heat the kitchen directly and partly to give poetry at least a chance. I read the flames assiduously and listen to the wood hiss and crack.

During the warmer months, I light a pine fire in a dilapidated iron hibachi grill outside the cabin, at a safe distance from Douglas the Fir. When I am lucky enough to have a fish, either bought in town or given to me by a neighbor who has a trout pond, or a splendid vegetable (red peppers, spring onions, aubergine, zucchini), the wood fire is the only real desideratum.

What winds up on my plate in December is prose, and poor prosaic prose at that. One dreams of summer at the supper table, and of alterations to my culinary lifestyle. If I could change one thing at the cabin, which I do not own, I would remove the electric plates and install a wood-burning stove, the kind where the smoke and flames roar through a snaky conduit that heats a stone bench in the stube, the stone bench that locals call a *Kunsht* (after the Latin *caustum*), before flying up the chimney. You cook at the stove, keep the dinner plates warm on the *Kunsht*, and afterward sit on a cushion at that same blessed place, where, because you ate so poetically, you doze. And you dream again of midsummer, although this time you dream like Shakespeare.

Platonism and Puritanism keep us on our spiritual toes

Thoreau reminds us of the seemingly ineradicable tradition of Platonism, which goes to meet the human body with contempt and a vigorous ascetic program. Platonism pervades Christian civilization down to our own age of secular postmodernism: the young man who eats only the expensive processed items that Arnold Schwarzenegger wants him to eat ("Vee vill pump you up!") and the young woman who is fighting her battle with anorexia or bulimia so that she may approximate to a state of nonbeing called Claudia Schiffer ("Vee vill pare you down!") are still caught up in that tyrannical Platonistic Puritanism that hates the body it disciplines. The fact that Schwarzenegger has replaced Plato, who in his youth was a wrestler, and that Schiffer has replaced Socrates, who drove the Athenian boys wild, means perhaps less than we think. And when newer models replace Schwarzenegger and Schiffer, the replacements have no effect on the underlying message.

The philosophers, it seems, and especially the Platonists, are responsible for this implacable Puritanism that will never give us peace. "Do not worry about the things of the body!" cries one of the neophyte converts to Brianism (in one of the two serious religious films ever produced, Monty Python's classic *The Life of Brian*), who then gets muddled and continues, "but about the things of the face and head!" A fine joke, because it is no joke at all. Consider the Puritan's feet and toes: the foot of the Platonistic Puritan extends from the toes and the sole (spell it right!) and heel to the hip, or perhaps all the way to the solar plexus, well above the gut wall. The "foot," in other words, includes all those parlous regions of the body that have to do with food, excretion, and sex. Which is of course—to cite the other serious religious film—the last temptation.

42

Neighbors, Part Four: Frau S.M.

She is so diffident that it's all she can do to step into a room full of people. Yet she has both brains and beauty in abundance, brains and beauty in that irresistible intertwined sort of way. She also has the smartest and most handsome husband in the village, two beautiful children, and a dozen beautiful grandchildren. We are inclined to say of a seventy-year-old woman who was once a great beauty that she has "aged well," as though she were a cabernet. Yet Frau S.M. is still a beauty, as are all persons who ever were truly beautiful.

—Beauty is fleeting! cries the preacher, whose stock in trade is loathsomeness.

As for Frau S.M., she is not only a beauty but also a kindly sorceress. She knows all the weeds of field and forest, and she knows the cures they proffer. She knows how to bake and construct a gingerbread house, like the house located deep in the shadowy forest that tempts hungry, unwary children. Frau S.M. bakes the best Linzer tart in the village, which is the tart with a choconutty crust and raspberry jam filling. She knows all about diet, in fact.

At a recent lecture in the village on the inspired dietetics of Hildegard of Bingen, a lecture preoccupied with flatulence and nightshade, full of strictures against this and that (including potatoes and strawberries, which, according to the pious Hildegard, are fouled by their proximity to the earth) and paeans to the other (such as the legumes that clamber toward heaven), I couldn't help but complain to this neighbor, who was sitting next to me.

—How can you be against potatoes? I asked.

Frau S.M. responded very quietly.

—A little bit of each thing: that is best.

Hildegard, incidentally, got her dietetics directly from God—in visions, it seems. She did not need a laboratory or a kitchen, but only a lively fancy warped by faith. It is good to know that the Father is so concerned about the flatulence of his children that he intervenes directly. By words, that is, and by epiphanies to Hildegard.

Frau S.M. got her dietetics and her pharmaceutical knowledge from her mother, her grandmother, and her Aunt Minnie, who delivered all the babies in the village for three or four generations. Perhaps it was Aunt Minnie who taught her niece so much about people too. Because I forgot to mention that when it comes to character, Frau S.M. has laser vision. I am a little bit afraid of her. I disrespect anyone who isn't a little bit afraid of her. Not exactly afraid. It's simply that we all crave this woman's respect, and we endeavor never to play the dunce in her presence.

Let's (*not!*) do lunch

Young people nowadays believe that the philosophers—all of them—are out to lunch. Yet the problem is that the philosophers have never been out to lunch. They have skipped the noonday meal and perhaps even breakfast, as Thoreau urges them all to do, lest rumination interfere with the life of the mind: "Let us rise early and fast, or break fast gently and without perturbation" (W 72). To break fast is perhaps a necessity, but to breakfast is merely to fall victim to a contraction. Yet worse awaits. Lunch, or "dinner," taken at noon, is sheer subservience: "Let us not be upset and overwhelmed in that terrible rapid and whirlpool called a dinner, situated in the meridian shallows. Weather this danger and you are safe, for the rest of the way is down hill. With unrelaxed nerves, with morning vigor, sail by it, looking another way, tied to the mast like Ulysses" (ibid.). Lunch, evidently, is a Siren, a snare—sexy but subversive.

—Let's *not* do lunch, Thoreau suggests.

—Let's *not* do breakfast, brunch, lunch, dinner, low tea, high tea, or supper, the Platonists suggested long before Thoreau.

With no snacks in between. Philosophy is preparation for dying and being dead—of hunger.

The perfect universe

But enough of Platonism. Let us look at a dialogue written by Plato himself instead. For sometimes the dialogues are hysterically funny. Plato's late dialogue *Timaeus* offers us a picture of the universe in which perfection requires self-sufficiency and the absence of all possible dependence on an "outside," especially an "outside" that might invade the "inside" as food. The Pythagorean astronomer who gives the dialogue *Timaeus* its name is absolutely clear about the threat represented by food. Yet his speech confronts the reader with a whole range of inconsistencies and baffling contradictions, many of them quite comical. The following passage tells us how the Demiurge fashioned the "perfect living body" of the universe:

> The living creature that was to contain all other living creatures within it had to assume a figure that would be appropriate for all the other figures. He therefore turned it about and made it into a sphere, . . . smoothing its surface everywhere quite perfectly, and this for many reasons. For it needed no eyes, since there was nothing visible, nor ears, for there was nothing audible left outside of it. Likewise there was no air surrounding it that it might breathe. (33b 1–33c 4)

Allow me to interrupt this tale of perfect interiority, where everything is inside. The living universe is to contain all other living creatures, albeit, presumably, without eating them. The round, smooth surface of the living universe indicates (among other things) that there is nothing outside that it could see with bulging Socratic eyes or hear with protruding Socratic ears. Indeed, there is no air out there that the living universe might breathe. The only unnerving question by this time is what it means to say that the universe is alive. What is life when there is nothing outside to inspire? But to continue:

> . . . also it needed no organ to take in nourishment, and no organ to remove from itself what it had previously taken in so as to suck the nourishing juices from it, because nothing was

excreted from it and nothing was added to it—inasmuch as there was no thing out there. Rather, the universe came to be through technical skill, in such a way that its excreta served as its nourishment, and in such a way that it suffered all things and performed all things in itself and on the basis of itself. For the one who fashioned it determined that it was better and more perfect for it to be self-sufficient than to be dependent on another. (33c 4–33d 3)

The main joke, of course, is the assertion that (1) there was nothing outside the universe that it could have eaten for breakfast *and* (2) its own excreta served as its nourishment. Excreta? Whence? From the unbroken fast? No food, no feces. Unless, of course, the main joke is that "there was no thing out there" except the Demiurge, on whom the self-sufficient universe was absolutely dependent—whereas independence is best.

There are other jokes about this perfect universe, such as the one about a living creature that is both technically "fashioned" and lovingly "conceived," both "made" and "generated," somehow "fabricated" by a craftsman who is also called "the father of the universe" (28c 3–4). Presumably, the father needed a woman to assist him in his "making," but Timaeus is agnostic on this delicate point. The Demiurge felt that autarchy was better than heterarchy, independence better than dependence. He must have known all about the imbroglios of dependence, however, inasmuch as when he came on the scene, the scene traditionally called "Chaos," Ananke was already there. Ananke? "Brute Necessity," the translators say. The Father and Demiurge "persuaded" Brute Necessity to cooperate in the making of the universe, says Timaeus, but once again he tells us nothing about the Demiurge's art of persuasion or the cosmogonic couple's "making it." The best lines in a comedy are always unspoken.

And so technical skill grapples with erotic necessity, manipulation mixes with natural process, doing seems indistinguishable from suffering, and both clone and kitten in this pukka universe unaccountably come to be. Timaeus's account is chock-full of odd dualisms, all of them derived from the great schism with which he begins, namely, the division between "being" (which is permanent, immutable, and perceived by the mind alone) and "becoming" (which is transitory, changeable, and perceived by the senses). Once being and coming-to-be are split in this way, the universe and the creatures in it will never be patched together again, and the jokes will continue to fly until Thoreau skips lunch and supper on the way to a nonsensual bedtime.

45

Autarchy; or, fatties beware!

Is Thoreau autarchic? Does he thrive on his own detritus? In a sense, yes, because like Plato he is a great writer. In any case, it is safe to say that Henry David Thoreau, perhaps like many other great writers, is ambivalent about food. Thoreau finds himself confronted by food everywhere in *Walden*, even though the subject always embarrasses him. Why? Because of the unity of the senses, he says, and the unity of our sensual nature. Eating is mixed up with sex, and both are contaminated by filth:

> I have found repeatedly, of late years, that I cannot fish without falling a little in self-respect. . . . [T]here is something essentially unclean about this diet and all flesh, and I began to see where housework commences, and whence the endeavor, which costs so much, to wear a tidy and respectable appearance each day, to keep the house sweet and free from all ill odors and sights. Having been my own butcher and scullion and cook, as well as the gentleman for whom the dishes were served up, I can speak from an unusually complete experience. The practical objection to animal food in my case was its uncleanness; and, besides, when I had caught and cleaned and cooked and eaten my fish, they seemed not to have fed me essentially. It was insignificant and unnecessary, and cost more than it came to. A little bread or a few potatoes would have done as well, with less trouble and filth. (W 163)

The life of the imagination—the life of the writer—demands abstinence, if not abstemiousness. At least the reputation of the potato has now been saved, but grosser forms of nourishment still must be avoided. *La nourriture, c'est la pourriture.* Better to be a butterfly sipping nectar than a caterpillar munching leaves. To say nothing of kittens chasing rodents. "The gross feeder is a man in the larva state; and there are whole nations in that condition, nations without fancy or imagination, whose vast abdomens betray them" (W 164). Imagine Thoreau strolling through the American megamall today, observing a whole nation of vast abdomens pushing shopping carts. He would not be kind.

46

Woodchuck Heaven

What about this ambivalence and embarrassment concerning victuals? In one breath Thoreau warns us, "put an extra condiment in your dish, and it will poison you," and then assures us, "for my part, I was never unusually squeamish" (W 164–65). A good part of Thoreau's repugnance, if not squeamishness, has to do with flesh, and no thinking person in our own time (thanks in part to the horrors of BSE or mad cow disease and the dissembling bureaucrats and agribusinessmen) can be unaffected by what Thoreau writes:

> It may be vain to ask why the imagination will not be reconciled to flesh and fat. I am satisfied that it is not. Is it not a reproach that man is a carnivorous animal? True, he can and does live, in a great measure, by preying on other animals, but this is a miserable way,—as any one who will go to snaring rabbits, or slaughtering lambs, may learn,—and he will be regarded as a benefactor of his race who shall teach man to confine himself to a more innocent and wholesome diet. Whatever my own practice may be, I have no doubt that it is a part of the destiny of the human race, in its gradual improvement, to leave off eating animals, as surely as the savage tribes have left off eating each other when they came in contact with the more civilized. (W 164)

In one breath, the sympathetic urge to stop killing other animals and the tendentious condemnation of the savage cannibal, who needs contact with the civilized world if he is ever to acknowledge "higher laws." We who glean Thoreau's text must be nervous eaters, too. "I could sometimes eat a fried rat with a good relish, if it were necessary," continues Thoreau, sinning against the proscriptions against both theriophagy and condiments. Yet the fried rat reminds us of one of the most hilarious moments in the Variorum edition of *Walden*. Thoreau has just informed us, with rhetorical zest, that he has dispatched a woodchuck from his beanfield to Woodchuck Heaven:

> The next year I sometimes caught a mess of fish for my dinner, and once I went so far as to slaughter a woodchuck which

ravaged my bean-field,—effect his transmigration, as a Tartar would say,—and devour him, partly for experiment's sake; but though it afforded me a momentary enjoyment, notwithstanding a musky flavor, I saw that the longest use would not make that a good practice, however it might seem to have your woodchucks dressed by the village butcher. (W 43)

The editor of the Variorum edition, who doubtless has donated his life's blood to Henry's cause, inserts a note after the phrase "slaughter a woodchuck" to assuage the wincing reader. The note (W 271n. 168) cites Henry Seidel Canby's *Thoreau* as the source of the following: "There is a pleasant little anecdote that Thoreau caught alive in a boxtrap one of the woodchucks that had been ravaging his beans. But not having the heart to kill it, he carted it off two miles and freed it, letting it be someone else's worry, not his own." Our editor neglects to note that the pesky, musky woodchuck continues to haunt Thoreau's imagination and his palate. "Higher Laws" begins as follows:

As I came home through the woods with my string of fish, trailing my pole, it being now quite dark, I caught a glimpse of a woodchuck stealing across my path, and felt a strange thrill of savage delight, and was strongly tempted to seize and devour him raw; not that I was hungry then, except for that wildness which he represented. Once or twice, however, while I lived at the pond, I found myself ranging the woods, like a half-starved hound, with a strange abandonment, seeking some kind of venison which I might devour, and no morsel could have been too savage for me. The wildest scenes had become unaccountably familiar. I found in myself, and still find, an instinct toward a higher, or, as it is named, spiritual life, as do most men, and another toward a primitive rank and savage one, and I reverence them both. I love the wild not less than the good. (W 160)

We recognize here Thoreau's image of himself as Hank the Hunk, brave chanticleer crowing lustily in mockery of "the good," "the reformers," "the do-gooders," jarring them out of their saccharine, moralizing complacency. Yet Hank the Hunk, or Henry the Hun, is really a slice of huckleberry pie. "Higher Laws" proceeds to the point at which we now stand, or wobble, somewhere downwind of the woodchuck. Thoreau sets aside coffee, tea, and wine ("wine is not so noble a liquor" [W 165]) and conjures up instead a "mental perception" of tastes—a higher, more spiritual apprehension of the gustatory—which would obviate the need for the grosser tongue. He forages for the berries (huckleberries and blueberries haunt his text as much as woodchucks do [see W 51, 130, 132, 166]) whose "ambrosial and essential part," namely, the "bloom," will feed his genius, not his gullet. He eschews, as he says, the "sensual savors" of the coarse provender destined for "the worms that possess us," hungering instead after images stored in the larder of the mind (W 166). Yet in the cases of both the savage hunter and the "fine lady" (ibid.) the challenge is the same: "The wonder is how they, how you and I, can live this slimy beastly life, eating and drinking" (ibid.).

Slimy beastly. Without a comma. Slithering toward us once again is the sinuous sensuous reptile that cajoled Eve and ruined Adam.

47

Mudslide Man

The next paragraph of "Higher Laws" begins: "Our whole life is startlingly moral. There is never an instant's truce between virtue and vice" (ibid.). Suddenly, inevitably, disappointingly, Cotton Mather begins to ventriloquize Thoreau's text, or at best Jonathan Edwards—or maybe Poor Richard: "Goodness is the only investment that never fails" (ibid.). We begin to understand why Herman Melville felt compelled to crow back at brave chanticleer in both *The Confidence-Man* and "Cock-A-Doodle-Doo," and why the wormy apple-tree table invoked at the end of *Walden* (W 251–52) induced such hilarity in Melville. Melville suspects that Hank the Hunk might simply have broken his digester. For "Higher Laws" turns out to be "a proud sweet satire on the meanness of our lives" (ibid.), as it moves predictably from excrementitiousness to sex. Or to the *absence* of sex. At all events, the progression (or regression, or mudslide) is from trophophobia, through scatophobia, to erotophobia:

> We are conscious of an animal in us, which awakens in proportion as our higher nature slumbers. It is reptile and sensual, and perhaps cannot be wholly expelled; like the worms which, even in life and health, occupy our bodies. Possibly we may withdraw from it, but never change its nature. I fear that it may enjoy a certain health of its own; that we may be well, yet not pure. The other day I picked up the lower jaw of a hog, with the white and sound teeth and tusks, which suggested that there was an animal health and vigor distinct from the spiritual. This creature succeeded by other means than temperance and purity. (W 167)

An insight worthy of Nietzsche—if only Thoreau had been able to sustain it. Yet he yearns for those nonsensuous savors of the spirit that spurn the wormy reptile and the healthy hog with equal animus. The only hope for humankind is what the psychoanalysts will soon be calling *sublimation*, taken in its most primitive form, namely, conserving "generative energy" by halting or redirecting its flow:

Yet the spirit can for the time pervade and control every member and function of the body, and transmute what in form is the grossest sensuality into purity and devotion. The generative energy, which, when we are loose, dissipates and makes us unclean, when we are continent invigorates and inspires us. Chastity is the flowering of man; and what are called Genius, Heroism, Holiness, and the like, are but various fruits which succeed it. Man flows at once to God when the channel of purity is open. By turns our purity inspires and our impurity casts us down. (Ibid.)

The sad alternation of upward and downward flows—one thinks of Augustine contrasting his heavenly Father's "milk" with the "birdlime of concupiscence" in himself—can end only in dejection. Humanity seems to have been cobbled together slapdash, a botched pastiche of bestiality and divinity. The fabled faun is wounded, sick, and dying: "He is blessed who is assured that the animal is dying out in him day by day, and the divine being established. Perhaps there is none but has cause for shame on account of the inferior and brutish nature to which he is allied. I fear that we are such gods or demigods only as fauns and satyrs, the divine allied to beasts, the creatures of appetite, and that, to some extent, our very life is our disgrace" (ibid.).

Our brutish nature, of brutish necessity, is our ignominy. Behind it all looms Ananke, "Brute Necessity," who baffled the Demiurge. "Brute Neighbors"? We have met them, and they are us. Better, or worse, they are the female parts in us. Our very *life* is our disgrace, and so we abandon ourselves to the good graces of *death*. Ananke? Whoever she is, wherever she is, she will always have been at fault. No Puritanism that is not also a misogyny.

Yet no matter how low "Higher Laws" go, Thoreau has his saving vices. After all, he wants to do little more in his life and in his writing than worship Nature. "We can never have enough of Nature," he cries in the peroration of his book—he who is daily surfeited with brutish nature (W 240). He affirms the "inviolable health of nature" even as he feels the worm at work in his belly and the stirrings of the reptile in the tropics. He proclaims the innocence of becoming, as though anticipating Nietzsche's rejoinder to Timaeus: "The impression made on a wise man is that of universal innocence" (ibid.). Talk of innocence, however, sometimes seems to be the mere rhetoric of peroration. We do see flashes of generosity throughout *Walden*, usually in those extended and generously detailed descriptions of nature. At the end of "Ponds," for example, Thoreau declares that human beings—and let us include all Puritans among them—are, fundamentally speaking, a bunch of ingrates: "Nature has no human inhabitant who appreciates her" (W 152). And at the beginning of "Solitude" we hear, "This is a delicious evening, when the whole body is one sense, and imbibes delight through every pore" (W 97). "Solitude" too has its peroration, invoking the faun, Great Pan, and Dame Nature, praising the "indescribable innocence and beneficence of Nature" (W 103). In "Solitude," Thoreau is less alone than ever: "Shall I not have intelligence with the earth? Am I not partly leaves and vegetable mould myself?" (W 104).

The mold soon molders, however, and Thoreau finds even the vernal vegetation of the spring hillside *grotesque* (W 230). Yet in the face of the impending mudslide, something powerfully affirmative in Thoreau's language, something like an imbibed or ingested delight, shows itself. It is language rapt to nature itself, language encrypted in the leaf and unfolding in the human body itself. Without citing Goethe's *Metamorphosis of Plants* (1790) directly, Thoreau provides a marvelous summary statement of its thesis (W 231–32). And his related account of the human body and face as richly lipped and lobed reminds us of an inspired passage in the German Romantic philosopher and poet Novalis, who offers us an account of what we might call Mr. Potato Head:

> Our lips often show great similarity to the two will-o'-the-wisps in [Goethe's] "Fairytale." The eyes are the higher pair of siblings to the lips. They close and open a holier grotto than the mouth. The ears are the serpent that hungrily swallows whatever the will-o'-the-wisps let fall. Mouth and eyes have a similar form. The lashes are the lips. The eyeball is the tongue and the gums, the pupil is the gorge. The nose is the mouth's brow, and the brow is the nose of the eyes. Each eye has a cheekbone as its chin. (CHV 2:557)

And here is Thoreau:

> What is man but a mass of thawing clay? The ball of the human finger is but a drop congealed. The fingers and toes flow to their extent from the thawing mass of the body. Who knows what the human body would expand and flow out to under a more genial heaven? Is not the hand a spreading *palm* leaf with its lobes and veins? The ear may be regarded, fancifully, as a lichen,

umbilicaria, on the side of the head, with its lobe or drop. The lip—*labium* from *labor* (?)—laps or lapses from the sides of the cavernous mouth.[1] The nose is a manifest congealed drop or stalactite. The chin is a still larger drop, the confluent dripping of the face. The cheeks are a slide from the brows into the valley of the face, opposed and diffused by the cheek bones. (W 232)

Mr. Potato Head meets Mudslide Man. Mudslide Man surprises us a bit, perhaps, with his lobes and labia, his globes and globules. On two different occasions in *Walden*, Thoreau confesses his fascination with the glottal and guttural phoneme *gl*. In his chapter on "Sounds," he writes of the hoot owl emitting "the dying moans of a human being,—some poor weak relic of mortality who has left hope behind, and howls like an animal, yet with human sobs, on entering the dark valley, made more awful by a certain gurgling melodiousness—I find myself beginning with the letters *gl* when I try to imitate it—expressive of a mind which has reached the gelatinous mildewy stage in the mortification of all healthy and courageous thought" (W 93). Mortification and mildew, yes, with all earth and flesh gone gelatinous—but still gurgling melodious in its language. The *gl* is heard once again in the hill's mudslide, where Thoreau etymologizes on *lobe* and *globe*, as though to undergird both Goethe's *Metamorphosis of Plants* and Jacques Derrida's *Glas*:

> No wonder that the earth expresses itself outwardly in leaves, it so labors with the idea inwardly. . . . *Internally*, whether in the globe or animal body, it is a moist thick *lobe*, a word especially applicable to the liver and lungs and the *leaves* of fat (λείβω, *labor, lapsus,* to flow or slip downward, a lapsing; λοβός, *globus,* lobe, globe; also lap, flap, and many other words,) *externally* a dry thin *leaf,* even as the *f* and *v* are a pressed and dried *b*. The radicals of lobe are *lb,* the soft mass of the *b* (single lobed, or B, double lobed,) with a liquid *l* behind it pressing it forward. In globe, *glb,* the guttural *g* adds to the meaning the capacity of the throat. The feathers and wings of birds are still drier and thinner leaves. Thus, also, you pass from the lumpish grub in the earth to the airy and fluttering butterfly. The very globe

---

1. The parenthetical question mark after the word *labor* is Thoreau's own; he is apparently worried about his etymology. Indeed, there seem to be two quite distinct forms of the word *labor* in Latin.

continually transcends and translates itself, and becomes winged in its orbit. (W 231)

From lumpish grub to guttural globe, Thoreau tests the capacity of the throat. He savors the sounds, rolls the words around on his tongue, engorges them as though for lunch, brings them up again, and spits them into winged orbit. Gleefully, I gloss this glandular glut of Thoreauvian glossolabia, not too glibly, I hope, because I continue to think of Derrida's *Glas*, which lucubrates on the guttural remains of language—the ineliminable orality of speech and phonetic writing. If we can gauge sensuality by the way one rolls those gelatinous, glutinous, lugubrious *gls* around on the tongue and up and down the throat, then Thoreau is one of the great American sensualists—which may not be saying a lot, but even so, people in *glas* houses shouldn't stone Thoreaus.

And yet the very muddy hillside that inspires the most glorious (or most grotesque) flowers of Thoreau's prose proves to be "somewhat excrementitious in its character" (W 233). And we are catapulted back onto "Higher Laws" and their lower implications for us all. We can never have enough of nature, according to Thoreau, and yet nature is too much of one lowly thing. Earlier on in *Walden*, we heard something about the unity of our senses and of sensuality, and it is high time to expand on this theme, in order then to bring this series of superfoetated aphorisms on food—after a brief reflection on beans—to a conclusion:

All sensuality is one, though it takes many forms; all purity is one. It is the same whether a man eat, or drink, or cohabit, or sleep sensually. They are but one appetite, and we only need to see a person do any one of these things to know how great a sensualist he is. The impure can neither stand nor sit with purity. When the reptile is attacked at one mouth of his burrow, he shows himself at another. If you would be chaste, you must be temperate. What is chastity? How shall a man know if he is chaste? He shall not know it. We have heard of this virtue, but we know not what it is. . . . If you would avoid uncleanness, and all the sins, work earnestly, though it be at cleaning a stable. Nature is hard to be overcome, but she must be overcome. (W 168)

Innocent, beneficent nature must be overcome, even if one should prove to be an ingrate by doing so. "Subdue and cultivate," as "Economy" tells us (W 44–47; 54). The perfect universe, lapsing into muck, needs to be purified, pyrified, and purged of its infinite imperfections.

Knowing beans

Twenty-seven cents a week—that is the essence of food, food as fuel, fueling the "Economy." Thoreau courts neither diet nor delight. Indian meal without yeast, a few potatoes, a few grains of rice, "a very little salt pork," molasses, "and salt, and my drink water" (W 44). "As simple a diet as the animals," writes Henry, boiling up his odoriferous purslane and sweet corn with a pinch of salt. Or perhaps rice, he adds, in honor of Hindu philosophy and mysticism, which assert themselves once again when Thoreau responds to critics of vegetarianism: "There is a certain class of unbelievers who sometimes ask me such questions as, if I think that I can live on vegetable food alone; and to strike at the root of the matter at once,—for the root is faith,—I am accustomed to answer such, that I can live on board nails" (W 47). Emerson's *Journals* attribute to Thoreau a similar formulation: "I like Henry Thoreau's statement on Diet: 'If a man does not believe that he can thrive on board nails, I will not talk with him'" (J 180). Brahman bed and board reduced to one trope. And speaking of tropes—

Thoreau wants to "suck out all the marrow of life," to live deliberately, and to simplify, above all by cutting down on his meals: "Instead of three meals a day, if it be necessary eat but one." (W 68). *If* it be necessary; otherwise, live like Timaeus's universe. At all events, marrow is the metaphor, even if the marrow is that of beans. Why does Thoreau want to grow beans? In order to *know* beans. A loyal Pythagorean, he cultivates them not for provender or profit but for paradox: he actually knows *beans* about beans. He engages with beans, he admits, "perchance, as some must work in fields if only for the sake of tropes and expressions, to serve a parable-maker one day" (W 122). A parable maker or a punster. What Thoreau wants most from food and the kitchen is, once again, *language*, even if it be language that contains two of the worst, most parlorous puns in the histories of the American and English tongues:

> It would seem as if the very language of our parlors would lose
> all its nerve and degenerate into *parlaver* wholly, our lives pass at
> such remoteness from its symbols, and its metaphors and tropes
> are necessarily so far fetched, through slides and dumb-waiters,

as it were; in other words, the parlor is so far from the kitchen and the workshop. The dinner even is only the parable of a dinner, commonly. As if only the savage dwelt near enough to Nature and Truth to borrow a trope from them. How can the scholar, who dwells away in the North West Territory or the Isle of Man, tell what is parliamentary in the kitchen? (W 186)

Let me stop complaining about punsters, however. People in glass houses. . . . Indeed, one could add condiment after condiment to these linguistic and literary concoctions and yet never ketchup with Henry. In any case, the stube clock has just struck noon. I must break now and go scramble up some tropes.

Tell Marlonbrando your dreams, honey, and everything will be all right, Part Three

—How can you have anything to do with an author who despises food and sensuality? Do you know what that says about you?

Marlonbrando intimidates me with his intensity. Our whole relationship revolves around food, and I can see that Thoreau is a threat to him. I feel the same threat.

—What can I say? He wants to suck the marrow out of life . . .

—He wants life on an autopsy table, growls Marlonbrando. What are you doing reading that sort of ilk?

—Don't be so judgmental!

Marlonbrando relents, although he is not happy. His hackles stand down, but he glowers left and right, seeking the composure that is his trademark.

—We'll come back to this. And we won't let nine lives pass before we do. Where were we?

—You were asking about the symmetry of the Bloomberry bush.

—Ah, yes, and your crazy Uncle Bill.

Marlonbrando mumbles almost inaudibly, now that he has regained his composure. He feigns nonchalance, picking absently at a piece of lint that has attached itself to the fur of his lapel. I rouse myself to defend my Uncle Bill, who was my godfather, after all, a role for which Marlonbrando should show some empathy.

—He wasn't crazy, just eccentric.

—This I have heard before.

—No, really, he was as sharp as a tack.

—I don't doubt it. You think crazies are stupid? They are the only ones who see the pickle we are in. But go on. Tell us about symmetry.

—My dad was remodeling the kitchen after the birth of his and my mom's first child. He was a civil engineer, and he had a good job, but times were tough.

—He suffered from depression?

—Yes, the Great Depression was still on, and so he did all the work on the house himself. What he was proudest of was the floor he laid in the kitchen—red and black asphalt tiles in a checkerboard pattern.

—Did he lay it out the way an engineer should?

—He did. He started in the middle of the floor, at the precise point where his two taut plumblines crossed.

—Were the walls of the house foursquare?

—It was an old house . . .

—Don't evade.

—You're taking Uncle Bill's side already!

—No, I'm not. I'm the disinterested observer. Go on.

—My dad did a perfect job. The floor looked great. My mom loved it.

—Of course she did.

—The floor was perfect. Why shouldn't she love it?

—Let's get to your Uncle Bill, shall we?

—They came to visit the house after my dad had finished the kitchen—crazy Uncle Bill and Aunt Catherine, my mom's oldest sister and my godmother.

—Your godmother married crazy Uncle Bill?

—Yes, she married him. All her sisters were appalled.

—Including your mother.

—Yes, mom too was appalled. It took all of them years to see how extraordinary a person he was, my crazy Uncle Bill, underneath all the eccentricity.

—This too I have heard before.

—You're not even interested in the story!

—Gripped. Fascinated. Go on, mutters Marlonbrando, still worrying that lint.

—Well, Uncle Bill examined the kitchen cabinets and was full of praise, looked over the new sink and registered approval. "What do you think of the floor?" asked my dad, unable to contain himself any longer. Crazy Uncle Bill cocked his head this way and that, got down on one knee, squinted at the checkerboard floor, examining it at all angles.

—Lacks symmetry, he said.

Moving mountains

I sit at my window and watch the mountains move. That is, from time to time I look up and see that they *have* moved—I never actually catch them in the act. They sometimes creep forward, advancing so close to the cabin that they seem but a flea hop away. And when I am distracted or otherwise occupied, they slip away, so far away that when I look up I see hours and hours of trekking to the horizon.

When a hole in the cloud cover allows the sun to shine on the snow-covered meadow outside my window, the mountains march boldly forward; when that hole closes and the mountains appear to be backlit, they curtsy and withdraw. If the wind has blown fiercely through the night, the mountains encroach; as the air becomes thicker or more humid in the course of the day, the mountains recede. I will say nothing about the effects of fog or falling snow or driving rain on the vagabond hills.

These are but the barest beginnings of a whole new science—the science of moving mountains. Geologists and geographers in times to come will name a goodly portion of the phenomena saved by this science after me, and I confess I am pleased by this prospect of immortality. I will spend it sitting industriously in front of my window, hoping someday to catch the mountains in the act, flagrante delicto.

Obscene spring

Thoreau says, as we heard a few moments ago, that the grassy embankment in spring is somewhat excrementitious, though some may doubt the existence of that word. Look at the colors of those wildflowers, see how they clash! I know a woman who manicures her garden in such a way that bright yellows and soft pinks never collide or even coincide, so nauseating would their combined impact be. The dandelions show no such compunction, to be sure, and they jostle the wild carnations and pink pinwheels for space; they are all looking for sex with bumblebees, I know, letting it all show, flaunting whatever color in the sun. Excrementitious or not, the dead land is indeed the soil that is breeding lilacs, and the exertions of spring, while cruel, are stupendous and stupefying. *The exertion of life.* Is that what makes the suicide rate soar in spring? Is that why so many, including my mother and father, die in the course of the cruelest month? Exertion, and not mere excrementition, is spring's glory and folly—the glory of obscene spring. Yet where is the poet or thinker who has not said this? I am only repeating what everyone knows or feels after they have spent weeks and months at hard labor, struggling to transform intransigent winter into rilly-dilly-ding time.

On jealousy and brutalization

There is much anger in *Walden*, along with touches of envy, but no jealousy. The last-named passion, or affect, or disease—this monster, green of eye and gill—seems to have left Thoreau unscathed. Does his agoraphobia rescue him from it? If no one gets close to him, all possible instances of jealousy seem to be ruled out from the start. At twenty-eight, Henry is the youngest old man of American letters. "I would rather sit on a pumpkin and have it all to myself, than be crowded on a velvet cushion. I would rather ride on earth in an ox cart with a free circulation, than go to heaven in the fancy car of an excursion train and breathe a *malaria* all the way" (W 26). I'm not sure whether the oxcart returns in *Walden*, but the pumpkin does, the second time only to be spurned: "None is so poor that he need sit on a pumpkin. That is shiftlessness" (W 48). Shiftlessness or agoraphobia? That appears to be the choice. In either case, Thoreau's philosophy of furniture is less ornate than Poe's, requiring only breathing room: "If we speak reservedly and thoughtfully, we want to be farther apart, that all animal heat and moisture may have a chance to evaporate" (W 106). Thoreau craves the cold and dry soul, which wants to be alone. What it requires is not a drawing room but a "withdrawing room" (ibid.). With all the others in withdrawal, there is no room for jealousy or any other intense affect.

Three pages in Thoreau's book separate the following two asseverations. First, "It would be better if there were but one inhabitant to a square mile, as where I live. The value of a man is not in his skin, that we should touch him" (W 102). Second, "I think that I love society as much as most, and am ready enough to fasten myself like a bloodsucker for a time to any full-blooded man that comes in my way" (W 105). Indeed, Thoreau sometimes seems as gregarious as Whitman on a Manhatto bus; he walks through the village for no reason other than "to see the men and boys" (W 127). Indeed, we learn from Emerson the highly improbable fact that Thoreau *admired* Whitman: "*Thoreau.* Perhaps his fancy for Walt Whitman grew out of his taste for wild nature, for an otter, a woodchuck, or a loon. He loved sufficiency, hated a sum that would not prove; loved Walt and hated Alcott" (J 424). Whitman or no, however, one has the sense that Thoreau is most comfortable on his solitary dusty pumpkin, most regal in his bumping oxcart, and most imperiously sovereign in his withdrawing room, secure from all the storms of passion. Secure, and yet impure. "Impure," vague, and troubled. At the end of "Higher Laws," Thoreau writes:

> I hesitate to say these things, but it is not because of the subject,—I care not how obscene my *words* are,—but because I cannot speak of them without betraying my impurity. We discourse freely without shame of one form of sensuality, and are silent about another. We are so degraded that we cannot speak simply of the necessary functions of human nature.
>
> Every man is the builder of a temple, called his body, to the god he worships, after a style purely his own, nor can he get off by hammering marble instead. We are all sculptors and painters, and our material is our own flesh and blood and bones. Any nobleness begins at once to refine a man's features, any meanness or sensuality to imbrute them. (W 168–69)

The one form of sensuality about which he discourses freely—albeit only to spurn it—is, as we have seen, that of eating. Of the other "necessary functions," the one sometimes involving cohabitation, sometimes not, remains without comment. No effort is made to distinguish it from "sleeping sensually." Nor does Thoreau note the compelling fact that none of these necessary functions seems to imbrute the brutes and that none of Thoreau's "Brute Neighbors" (that is the title of the next chapter of *Walden*) are caught engaging in sensual sleep. Neither mouse nor loon nor even the warring ants ("I have no doubt that it was a principle they fought for" [W 175]) appear to have been imbruted—unless by their contact with humanity.

Thoreau constructs the temple of his flesh not after a style wholly his own, however, but out of the dilapidated moralizing dictates of our tradition. There is no psychology in Thoreau's book, hence, no serious ethics. (His geometry of ethics, complete with the classic and commonplace sort of phrenology that such geometries love to produce [W 220] is an embarrassment.) And without a psychology there is no account of the passions, affects, and emotions—all those things Thoreau disdains in favor of pond ice. If only he had dared to wonder whether it is in fact the icy intellect that brutalizes humanity.

Yet why ask about jealousy in particular? Why not some more positive and hygienic affect? Because even after we have learned to sleep sensually in the temple, and even to cohabit there, making churchgoing a less sterile affair than we were raised to believe it had to be, the fit of jealousy—a fit that knows full well how to let icy intellect do all the work of projection and vilification—sometimes fills us with a self-loathing powerful enough to blast any possible psychology. Who can bear to be exposed as the absurdly jealous lover, the ridiculously jealous competitor, the panicky ingrate who digs his lonely grave and leaps into it? Who wants to play the fool, the dupe, the Othello who punishes his friends and lovers, repaying their generosity with suspicion and paranoia? Jealousy strangles all the gentle daemons and fair Desdemona's of the soul.

There are affects we must fear as much as Thoreau fears sensual sleep, affects that do not imbrute us only because the brutes are often more humane than we are. The jealous lover brutalizes his love and his self; that is to say, he *humanizes* them by thinking all things through in a supremely rational manner, rehearsing them, calculating the loss and the chagrin—*she is with him now, they have returned to her place, see how she kisses him, and where are his hands? the beast! both of them, beasts!* Jealousy is human enough to define the human, now that the "rational animal" of traditional philosophy is done for. Jealousy is human, all-too-human, as Nietzsche says, agreeing with Aristotle: one can be mortally jealous even of the dead, as Xenophanes was said to have been insanely jealous of old Homer. When an animal has lost pride of place and slips from alpha to beta, it learns how to walk away and let the species prevail. It does not gnaw on the bones of rancor, resentment, and jealousy. If only we humans were so clever. For if we could adequately imbrute ourselves, that is, imbue ourselves with animal *Gelassenheit*, or "letting-be," we and all the other animals we know and love would be better off.

The bowlegged larch

A conifer, but deciduously not an evergreen. The larch stands about five meters upwind from the cabin and soars almost as high as Douglas the Fir. What is distinctive about my larch is that its trunk is bowed. The first six meters lean far to the east, having grown up under the constant harassment of the west wind and the enticement of the morning sun. After that, having gained confidence and a foothold, the larch grew as straight as an arrow. The problem is that from inside the cabin, where I watch the thunderstorms, I can see only the first six meters of the trunk. Lightning illumines the earth so eerily at two or three in the morning that I think I am already in the netherworld. The wind has already howled me into wakefulness, and I have climbed down the stairs and entered the stube. From there I watch the storm like an ancient Athenian spellbound at the Theatre of Dionysos. The cabin shudders under the impact of the wind. When I look out the window of the south wall, the swaying trunk of the bowlegged larch seems destined to uproot and crash down onto the cabin, sweeping me off to what Hölderlin called the ex-centric realm of the dead. Yet it is only an illusion. The larch is deeply rooted, the forester assures me. It will not fall. Only its bowleggedness makes it seem to bend so impossibly low under the force of the wind that it will soon reach the breaking point. And if it were to snap? For I have seen gigantic trees spin in a stormwind like dervishes, then suddenly snap like matchsticks. The larch is my *Prometheus Bound* and my *Being and Time*. I need no other witness to my mortality. If only all the heralds of death were merely bowlegged, merely cute!

54

Speculative gardening

Atop Schauinsland Mountain, in view of the Feldberg, the highest mountain of the Black Forest, you scratch the surface of the earth and your fingernails come up with beach sand—evidence that the entire Black Forest mountain chain was heaved up from the Mediterranean basin by dint of the Libyan Plate crashing into whatever it was that became Italy. Two to four million years ago? Something like that. Paleontologists concede that after a few hundred thousands of years, our minds lose track and the numbers merely numb us. Yet, sure enough, it is sand, grit under the nails, even if by this time it has lost all smack of salt. (The Germans say *Geschmack* for "smack," one of the loveliest words in both our languages. In English, it used to be the sound or perhaps the result of planting a kiss, but now it's an illegal substance, I believe.) The imagination cannot comprehend all those years—the mathematical sublime—and so resorts to either the science of paleontology or smack, depending on one's taste. Yet it is good from time to time to climb a hill, scratch the surface of the earth, and engage in speculative gardening.

55

Former inhabitants

The village of Sankt Ulrich is growing. There are now some 450 inhabitants, not counting the cows, goats, chickens, and wild things, but including me. In the village cemetery that skirts the church lie the former inhabitants. There is room for them for only three generations, after which they are exhumed and space made for more recent members of the family. (What is done with that exhumed and moldering earth? you may ask me, but I do not know. I hope it goes to the nursery down the road; farm people like to be of use.) Scattered across the following pages is a rogues' gallery of a few of the valley's former inhabitants, starting with one who was no rogue at all, Frau J.

She wore dark glasses indoors and out. She was almost totally blind. Yet Frau J. spent her last years spinning wool sheared from her own sheep. White, gray, beige, and dark brown wool from the different breeds. The sheep dotted the side of Wintry Hill, where she and her husband inhabited a tiny cottage that has since given way to a larger and less impressive house. She taught the younger women in the village how to spin the carded wool, then take two of the thin threads and spin them in the opposite direction. *Zwirnen*, or "twining," is the name of the second process. The result of this redoubled, reversed spinning is a very tough strand of wool, ready for weaving or knitting. There is a popular expression here that runs, in translation, "Heaven, my ass, and twine!" I am uncertain about its meaning and derivation, although the speculations among linguists are delightful. One of my best friends here in Germany uses the expression all the time—"Heaven, my ass, and twine!"—and I never know what he means by it, although I am certain that something has excited him. Once the yarn has been double-spun, it is well-nigh unbreakable. The sweaters that the young women knitted from Frau J.'s wool lasted forty years and more with a minimum of care. They are still worn today. And they keep about them that smoky, gamy, comforting smell of the sheep that grazed decades ago on Wintry Hill.

The two corners of Melville's smile

Something of a Nietzschean boastfulness—"Surely, I am flame!"—is audible in Thoreau's remark, cited by Emerson from an unpublished manuscript of Thoreau's: "I ask to be melted. You can only ask of the metals that they be tender to the fire that melts them. To nought else can they be tender" (SW 428). And this, recorded in Emerson's *Journals* for the year 1852: "Henry Thoreau rightly said, the other evening, talking of lightning-rods, that the only rod of safety was in the vertebrae of his own spine" (J 369). Emerson often finds Thoreau captious, irascible, unyielding, even curmudgeonly. Yet that is not the worst, not Henry's least pleasant side. His least pleasant side is the one that loves to brag. It is the side that Herman Melville couldn't help but satirize; indeed, he satirized it so well that one is secretly grateful for Thoreau's braggadocio.

Thoreau begins and ends his book on Walden Pond by crowing, and he crows throughout the middle sections of the book as well. Chanticleer rouses his neighbors from their dogmatic slumber, and he clearly loves the sound of his own crowing. Here is the book's motto, set in small capitals, as though Thoreau means it to be heard reverberating through the hills of Concord and environs:

I DO NOT PROPOSE TO WRITE AN ODE TO DEJECTION, BUT TO BRAG AS LUSTILY AS CHANTICLEER IN THE MORNING, STANDING ON HIS ROOST, IF ONLY TO WAKE MY NEIGHBORS UP.

In case the somnolent reader has overlooked the motto, Thoreau repeats his words in the chapter entitled "Where I Lived, and What I Lived For" (W 62). Later, in "Sounds," Thoreau hears the cock's crow once again, and he celebrates its call as though it were his own:

The note of this once wild Indian pheasant is certainly the most remarkable of any bird's, and if they could be naturalized without being domesticated, it would soon become the most famous sound in our woods, surpassing the clangor of the goose and the hooting of the owl; and then imagine the cackling of the hens to fill the pauses when their lords' clarions rested! No wonder that man added this bird to his tame stock,—to say nothing of the eggs and drumsticks. To walk in a winter morning in a wood where these birds abounded, their native woods, and hear the wild cockerel crow on the trees, clear and shrill for miles over the resounding earth, drowning the feebler notes of other birds,—think of it! It would put nations on the alert. Who would not be early to rise, and rise earlier and earlier every successive day of his life, till he became unspeakably healthy, wealthy, and wise? This foreign bird's note is celebrated by the poets of all countries along with the notes of their native songsters. All climates agree with brave Chanticleer. He is more indigenous even than the natives. His health is ever good, his lungs are sound, his spirits never sag. (W 95)

Thoreau's *Walden* goes on to reproduce the crowing of brave chanticleer as often as it can: our author needs no domestic sounds to keep him sane; he needs no birds for his yard, for he has no bounded and hedged yard at all; "—no gate—no front yard,—and no path to the civilized world!" (W 96). The crowing continues in *Walden's* next chapter, "Solitude," but that need not detain us here. Suffice it to say that one is never sure whether Thoreau is proud to be alone or alone to be proud. "I have, as it were, my own sun and moon and stars, and a little world all to myself. . . . [A]nd the black kernel of the night was never profaned by any human neighborhood" (W 98).

Now, Herman Melville, surrounded by his wife and many children, may have been more profoundly alone than Thoreau ever was. Or, if that is unfair, or undecidable, then he was surely Thoreau's equal in solitude. Yet he also knew how to puncture the inflated solitude that is so full of itself that it counts for all the company in the world. "Cock-A-Doodle-Doo!" is the title of Melville's story, with the subtitle, "The Crowing of the Noble Cock Beneventano." Melville manages to subvert Thoreau's image of chanticleer while at the same time mimicking Thoreau's braggadocio to perfection. Melville's narrator opens with a reflection on feisty rebellion against despotism, technical progress, and the banks, as his morning walk discloses to him on all sides a diseased nature. "Yea, what's the use of bothering the very heavens about it? Don't the heavens themselves ordain these things—else they could not happen?" (PT 269). The narrator continues to grumble about a creditor whose dun is hounding him for payment, about his dyspepsia, and about the filth pasted to the flanks of the scrawny calves

105

who have been sprawling in the barn all winter long, calves who look more like trunks made of hirsute cowhide than living creatures. He grumbles about the universe in general and life in particular, when a cock's crow transmutes all his grumbles to glory:

> Hark! By Jove, what's that? See! the very hair-trunks prick their ears at it, and stand and gaze away down into the rolling country yonder. Hark again! How clear! how musical! how prolonged! What a triumphant thanksgiving of a cock-crow! *"Glory be to God in the highest!"* It says those very words as plain as ever cock did in this world. . . . *"Never say die!"* My friends, it is extraordinary, is it not? (PT 271)

"Never say die," the cock seems to cry. Yet at the climax of the story someone dies each time the cock crows. "Glory in the highest," says our smitten narrator. Yet he has already admonished us that heaven itself ordains "the universal spell of tribulation" on earth. Melville himself makes ironic reference to Emersonian "self-reliance" and Socratic optimism, the "invincible" Socrates being "the game-fowl Greek" who offered a cock to Asclepius and "died unappalled" (PT 275). Yet there are also several cryptic references to Thoreau. First, the owner of the Shanghai rooster is named "Merrymusk," a name that reminds us of Thoreau's week on the Concord and Merrimack Rivers. Second, and third, there are some wordplays that allow us to hear the name *Thoreau* in Melville's text:

> I had heard plenty of cock-crows before, and many fine ones;— but this one! so smooth and flute-like in its very clamor—so self-possessed in its very rapture of exultation—so vast, mounting, swelling, soaring, as if spurted out from a golden throat, thrown far back. . . . It was wise crow; an invincible crow; a philosophic crow; a crow of all crows. (PT 274)

". . . a golden thoreaut, thoreaun far back"? Can Melville be guilty of such risible puns? I would be the last to accuse him or anyone else, of course. Yet Melville has his narrator reading *Tristram Shandy* when the creditor's dun comes calling, so that when it comes to puns, anything is possible. And, as if once were not enough, Melville repeats the possible wordplay a few pages later: "My soul, too, would turn chanticleer, and clap her wings, and throw back her throat" (PT 278). The cock, Beneventano, seems "in a rapture of benevolent delight" (PT 287). But each time he crows, one of the

Merrymusk children dies, until, after one particularly lusty blast, the cock himself expires. Our narrator buries the rooster and all the Merrymusks, chiseling Paul's famous taunt on their common gravestone: "*O death, where is thy sting? O grave, where is thy victory?*" The answer to Paul's taunt, of course, lies as deep as the collective grave that the narrator has scraped "nigh the railroad track" and "on the other side of the swamp," a grave as deep as the parodic optimism of the story's close:

> . . . and never since then have I felt the doleful dumps, but under all circumstances crow late and early with a continual crow. Cock-a-doodle-doo!—oo!—oo!—oo!—oo! (PT 288)

At the very end of *Walden*, Thoreau trades in his rooster for a bug, but the message is the same, and Melville will proffer the same response. Here is Thoreau:

> Every one has heard the story which has gone the rounds of New England, of a strong and beautiful bug which came out of the dry leaf of an old table of apple-tree wood, which had stood in a farmer's kitchen for sixty years, first in Connecticut, and afterward in Massachusetts,—from an egg deposited in the living tree many years earlier still, as appeared by counting the annual layers beyond it; which was heard gnawing out for several weeks, hatched perchance by the heat of an urn. Who does not feel his faith in a resurrection and immortality strengthened by hearing of this? (W 251–52)

Who does not? Melville and his Merrymusks, among others, do not. Melville has the hero of "The Apple-Tree Table; or, Original Spiritual Manifestations" discovering the table in the garret of an old haunted house he and his family have newly occupied. The garret is itself a graveyard of buggy spiritual manifestations, with the narrator espying in its "dense curtain of cobwebs . . . in funereal accumulations . . . from the groined, murky ceiling . . . as in aerial catacombs, myriads of all tribes of mummified insects" (PT 379). It does not take long for the narrator to establish the Thoreauvian transcendentalist metaphor: "As from the gloom of the grave and the companionship of worms, man shall at last rapturously rise into the living greenness and glory immortal" (PT 380) Thoreau's warm urn is there, and it is joined by other tepid and cushy things, "with all the kindly influences of warm urns, warm fires, and warm hearts" (PT 381). While his shrewish wife scolds and his flighty daughters (accompanied by Biddy, the superstitious Catholic maid) have visions of spirits dancing in their heads, our narrator reads Democritus and tries to be as skeptical and urbane as the ancient atomist reputedly was. After a nerve-racking couple of weeks, during which the bug noisily munches its way to the surface of the table, science wins the day: the bug, glowing like a ghostly opal, is estimated to have been one hundred and fifty years in the egg, and the phenomenon of its "resurrection" is adjudged an entirely natural—not a supernatural— affair. Thoreau celebrates a secret victory at the end of Melville's "Apple-Tree Table," however, as the marvel of life brings the spirit world back to immanence and the earth. The elder daughter speaks:

> "Say what you will," said Julia, holding up, in the covered tumbler, the glorious, lustrous, flashing live opal, "say what you will, if this beauteous creature be not a spirit, it yet teaches a spiritual lesson. For if, after one hundred and fifty years' entombment, a mere insect comes forth at last into light, itself an effulgence, shall there be no glorified resurrection for the spirit of man? Spirits! spirits!" she exclaimed, with rapture, "I still believe in spirits, only now I believe in them with delight, when before I but thought of them in terror." (PT 397)

As for the narrator himself, however, he cannot refrain from adding an ironic twist to his daughter's rapturous speech: "The mysterious insect did not long enjoy its radiant life; it expired the next day. But my girls have preserved it. Embalmed in a silver vinaigrette, it lies on the little apple-tree table in the pier of the cedar-parlor" (PT 397). So much for original, now pickled, spiritual manifestations. The beginning and the end of Thoreau's *Walden*, from cock's crow to opalescent bug, serve to elevate the two corners of Melville's wry and rueful smile.

57

Thaw and Thor

It would be lovely if we could say of Thoreau what he says of spring as opposed to winter: "Thaw[reau?] with his gentle persuasion is more powerful than Thor[eau?] with his hammer" (W 233). Indeed, with the author himself juxtaposing Thaw and Thor, we may suspect that he genuinely favors "gentle persuasion," no matter how much he huffs and puffs and crows.

However, before we satisfy ourselves that winter is done for, that Thor is about to melt with fellow feeling, one more word about snowstorms at the cabin, which can come anytime between early October and late April. The winter wind is the most impressive of all the winds and not simply because of its contribution to the cold. If there is fresh snow on the ground, the wind can whip it up and create a Sahara sandstorm out of fallen flakes, building and destroying dunes like a god playing with the dust of the primeval world. The flakes turn into razor-sharp projectiles that sting your face. And the wind can blow you away. I recall a January storm when the path to the cabin, up at the Storm Beech, was solid ice from earlier thaws

and refreezings. Walking on the ice, crouching in the wind, I was blown off my feet three or four times, until I realized that I could make progress only by crawling on my hands and knees. That put me below the main blast of the wind. When I made it to the cabin, I recounted my canine adventure to my daughter Salomé Maria who was visiting at the time.

She received my story with skepticism. I invited her to put on her coat and join in the experiment. We made it up to the Storm Beech fine, but when it was time to turn about and head for home, there were suddenly two poochies on the path. After a long crawl, we rewarded ourselves with nonskeptical hot chocolate.

Former inhabitants, Part Two

Herr L. did not so much ask for rides into town as extort them. He would come and sit on the bench by your front door, and when you came out to tend to whatever business you had to attend to, he would announce to you your first destination, which was wherever he wanted to go. He loved practical jokes, and he was mean to his wife. (Apologies for the redundancy.) One morning, he obeyed the call of an old village tradition and hanged himself from the main rafter of the barn, knowing that his wife would discover him at milking time. She did. Local wisdom says that he had two wives and that he played this little prank on both of them, but that is probably an exaggeration.

Taking the arm of an elm tree

"He was a born protestant," writes Emerson in his obsequy for Thoreau, "a protestant *à l'outrance*" (SW 413). Yet in Emerson's view the otherwise admirable, laudable, iconoclastic protestant occasionally protested too much:

> There was somewhat military in his nature not to be subdued, always manly and able, but rarely tender, as if he did not feel himself except in opposition. He wanted a fallacy to expose, a blunder to pillory, I may say required a little sense of victory, a roll of the drum, to call his powers into full exercise. It cost

him nothing to say No; indeed, he found it much easier than to say Yes. It seemed as if his first instinct on hearing a proposition was to controvert it, so impatient was he of the limitations of our daily thought. This habit, of course, is a little chilling to the social affections; and though the companion would in the end acquit him of any malice or untruth, yet it mars conversation. Hence, no equal companion stood in affectionate relations with one so pure and guileless. "I love Henry," said one of his friends, "but I cannot like him; and as for taking his arm, I should as soon think of taking the arm of an elm-tree." (SW 414–15; cf. J 375)

In his *Journals*, Emerson is more candid: it is not some "friend" who adds the remark about the arm of an elm tree, but Emerson himself (J 326; cf. 255). Robert Louis Stevenson remarks somewhere that it was no accident that Thoreau cultivated successful relationships with fish. Emerson notes that no human being was able to conceal any form of foolishness "from such terrible eyes" as Thoreau's (SW 419). Even the august institutions of higher learning, the colleges, "feared the satire of his presence" (SW 423). Hence, words like *austerity* and *severity* fall over and over again in Emerson's paean to his deceased friend:

His virtues, of course, sometimes ran into extremes. It was easy to trace to the inexorable demand on all for exact truth that austerity which made this willing hermit more solitary even than he wished. . . . Such dangerous frankness was in his dealing that his admirers called him "that terrible Thoreau," as if he spoke when silent, and was still present when he had departed. I think the severity of his ideal interfered to deprive him of a healthy sufficiency of human society. (SW 426)

When we sample Emerson's *Journals*, we get a sense of both the admirable and the abrasive Thoreau. The result of such a sampling is a heady bouquet, one that evokes both esteem and allergy. From the year 1838: "My good Henry Thoreau made this else solitary afternoon sunny with his simplicity and clear perception. How comic is simplicity in this double-dealing, quacking world. Everything that boy says makes merry with society, though nothing can be graver than his meaning" (J 97). From 1839: "My brave Henry here who is content to live now, and feels no shame in not studying any profession, for he does not postpone his life, but lives,

114

already,—pours contempt on these crybabies of routine and Boston. He has not one chance but a hundred chances" (J 146–47).

Then, four years later, in 1843, more critically: "Young men, like Henry Thoreau, owe us a new world, and they have not acquitted the debt. For the most part, such die young, and so dodge the fulfilment. One of our girls said, that Henry never went through the kitchen without coloring" (J 255). Why coloring? Because of the presence of women in the kitchen? Is Thoreau's diffidence part of the dodge? Emerson does not say. At all events, that same year: "Henry Thoreau sends me a paper with the old fault of unlimited contradiction. The trick of his rhetoric is soon learned: it consists in substituting for the obvious word and thought its diametrical antagonist. . . . Channing declared the piece is excellent: but it makes me nervous and wretched to read it, with all its merits" (J 267). A year later, in 1844:

> Henry Thoreau's conversation consisted of a continual coining of the present moment into a sentence and offering it to me. I compared it to a boy, who, from the universal snow lying on the earth, gathers up a little in his hand, rolls it into a ball, and flings it at me. . . . Henry is . . . not encumbered with himself. He has no troublesome memory, no wake, but lives *ex tempore*, and brings to-day a new proposition as radical and revolutionary as that of yesterday, but different. The only man of leisure in the town. . . . [H]e has declined all the kingdoms of this world. Satan has no bribe for him. (J 277)

Three years later, in 1847: "Thoreau sometimes appears only as a *gendarme*, good to knock down a cockney with, but without that power to cheer and establish which makes the value of a friend" (J 311). In 1848: "Henry Thoreau is like the wood-god who solicits the wandering poet and draws him into antres vast and desarts idle, and bereaves him of his memory, and leaves him naked, plaiting vines and with twigs in his hand. I spoke of friendship but my friends and I are fishes in our habit" (J 325–26). Fishes? Shades of Stevenson!

Four years later, in 1852, once again admiringly: "Thoreau gives me, in flesh and blood and pertinacious Saxon belief, my own ethics. He is far more real, and daily practically obeying them, than I; and fortifies my memory at all times with an affirmative experience which refuses to be set aside" (J 370). In 1854, full of awe: "Henry Thoreau charged [his friend Harrison] Blake, if he could not do hard tasks, to take the soft ones, and when he liked anything, if it was only a picture or a tune, to stay by it, find out what he liked, and draw that sense of meaning out of it, and do *that*: harden it, somehow and make it his own. Blake thought and thought on this, and wrote afterwards to Henry, that he had got his first glimpse of heaven. Henry was a good physician" (J 378). In 1856, full of exasperation:

> If I knew only Thoreau, I should think coöperation of good men impossible. Must we always talk for victory, and never once for truth, for comfort, and joy? Centrality he has, and penetration, strong understanding, and the higher gifts,—the insight of the real, or from the real, and the moral rectitude that belongs to it; but all this and all his resources of wit and invention are lost to me, in every experiment, year after year, that I make, to hold intercourse with his mind. Always some weary captious paradox to fight you with, and the time and temper wasted. (J 391–92)

That same year, with equal exasperation: "It is curious that Thoreau goes to a house to say with little preface what he has just read or observed, delivers it in lump, is quite inattentive to any comment or thought which any of the company offer on the matter, nay, is merely interrupted by it, and when he has finished his report departs with precipitation" (J 393).

Later that same year, while accompanying Thoreau on a trip through the latter's natural habitat, where no "company" dares to offer "comment," Emerson notes: "Yesterday to the Sawmill Brook with Henry. He was in search of yellow violets which he waded into the water for; and which he concluded, on examination, had been out five days. Having found his flowers, he drew out of his breast pocket his diary and read the names of all the plants which should bloom on this day, May 20; whereof he keeps account as a banker when his notes fall due." Emerson's lengthy account of Thoreau as a naturalist continues, after a small break, as follows: "There came Henry with music-book under his arm, to press flowers in; with telescope in his pocket, to see the birds, and microscope to count stamens; with a diary, jack-knife, and twine; in stout shoes, and strong grey trousers, ready to brave the shrub oaks and smilax, and to climb the tree for a hawk's nest. His strong legs, when he wades, were no insignificant part of his armour" (J 395–96). Then, the next year, 1857: "Henry avoids commonplace, and talks birch bark to all comers, reduces them all to the same insignificance" (J 403). Birch bark is noted for its astringency; the birch twig, when multiplied, goes to make a broom or a schoolmaster's switch.

In 1862, not long before Thoreau's death on May 6, Emerson reports the words of a visitor to Thoreau's deathbed: "Sam Staples yesterday had been to see Henry Thoreau. 'Never spent an hour with more satisfaction. Never saw a man dying with so much pleasure and peace.' Thinks that very few men in Concord know Mr. Thoreau; finds him serene and happy" (J 425). That same year, but after Thoreau's death:

> Henry Thoreau remains erect, calm, self-subsistent, before me, and I read him not only truly in his Journal, but he is not long out of mind when I walk, and, as to-day, row upon the pond. He chose wisely no doubt for himself to be the bachelor of thought and nature that he was,—how near to the old monks in their ascetic religion! He had no talent for wealth, and knew how to be poor without the least hint of squalor or inelegance. Perhaps he fell—all of us do—into his way of living, without forecasting it much, but approved and confirmed it with later wisdom. (J 426)

Then, after a paragraph break, Emerson appears to telegraph a reply to my complaint about Thoreau's braggadocio: "If there is a little strut in the style of Henry, it is only from a vigour in excess of the size of his body" (ibid.). Thoreau as a Napoleon of the pen? Perhaps Caesar ought to have said, "I would that he were *taller*."

Finally, in the following year, 1863, the most generous entry—the one with which we may conclude our sampling:

> In reading Henry Thoreau's journal, I am very sensible of the vigour of his constitution. That oaken strength which I noted whenever he walked, or worked, or surveyed woodlots, the same unhesitating hand with which a field-labourer accosts a piece of work, which I should shun as a waste of strength, Henry shows in his literary task. He has muscle, and ventures on and performs feats which I am forced to decline. In reading him, I find the same thought, the same spirit that is in me, but he takes a step beyond, and illustrates by excellent images that which I should have conveyed in a sleepy generality. 'T is as if I went into a gymnasium, and saw youths leap, climb, and swing with a force unapproachable,—though their feats are only continuations of my initial grapplings and jumps. (J 432)

Is there anyone else who so challenges Emerson's undisputed leadership of the Transcendentalists? Is there anyone—besides Whitman—whom Emerson admires beyond the outermost limits of envy? Is there anyone who so tries and tests Emerson's love of companionability? One has the feeling that, whatever the happenstances of chronology and biography, Emerson is always and everywhere in his essays on "Love" and "Friendship" writing about Thoreau. For example, in this sudden vision of "Love": "Behold there in the wood the fine madman! he is a palace of sweet sounds and sights; he dilates; he is twice a man; he walks with arms akimbo; he soliloquizes; he accosts the grass and trees; he feels the blood of the violet, the clover and the lily in his veins; and he talks with the brook that wets his foot."

Thoreau's serviceable body

Emerson is kinder about Thoreau's Puritanism and asceticism than I have been, and one of the most remarkable passages in his eulogy of Thoreau touches on Thoreau's body and Thoreau's *relation* to his body. I quote it in full:

> It was said of Plotinus that he was ashamed of his body, and 't is very likely he had good reason for it,—that his body was a bad servant, and he had not skill in dealing with the material world, as happens often to men of abstract intellect. But Mr. Thoreau was equipped with a most adapted and serviceable body. He was of short stature, firmly built, of light complexion, with strong, serious blue eyes, and a grave aspect,—his face covered in the late years with a becoming beard. His senses were acute, his frame well-knit and hard, his hands strong and skilful in the use of tools. And there was a wonderful fitness of body and mind. He could pace sixteen rods more accurately than another man could measure them with rod and chain. He could find his path in the woods at night, he said, better by his feet than his eyes. He could estimate the measure of a tree very well by his eye; he could estimate the weight of a calf or a pig, like a dealer. From a box containing a bushel or more of loose pencils, he could take up with his hands fast enough just a dozen pencils at every grasp. He was a good swimmer, runner, skater, boatman, and would probably outwalk most countrymen in a day's journey. And the relation of body to mind was still finer than we have indicated. He said he wanted every stride his legs made. The length of his walk uniformly made the length of his writing. If shut up in the house, he did not write at all. (SW 417)

It is intriguing that a man so opposed to slavery holds his own body in such bondage to tasks. Intriguing too that this reduction of the human body to skills and functions and bravura performances still dominates the

US-American psyche, which in spite of all the raunchy gab fears above all else the body as a possible site of pleasure.

And my own body? Do not I too hold it in bondage to tasks, even if the principal task is to sit for unconscionably long periods of time, reading and writing and ruining my posture? Is it not always a series of fortunate accidents and interruptions that bring my body pleasure? Do I not always seek out mere loopholes in the Law of the Pleasure Principle? The forces that rule in Henry are not powerless in me.

On loneliness; or, snap out of it!

Thoreau declares: "I have never felt lonesome, or in the least oppressed by a sense of solitude, but once, when for an hour, I doubted if the near neighborhood of man was not essential to a serene and healthy life" (W 99). Emerson's journal entry of October 27, 1851, makes more sense to me, and it exposes Thoreau's braggadocio: "It would be hard to recall the rambles of last night's talk with H. T. But we stated over again, to sadness, almost, the eternal loneliness. . . . How insular and pathetically solitary, are all the people we know" (SW 153–54). To sadness, almost. One page prior to Thoreau's declaration that he has felt lonesome only once in his life we read: "Nothing can rightly compel a simple and brave man to a vulgar sadness" (W 98).

A vulgar sadness? What is that? To be sad the way the crowd is sad? And what is wrong with that, especially for those of us who grew up in the lonely crowd? A simple and brave man? Perhaps I am not simple enough? No doubt, I am not brave; never was. Melville was brave. In *Pierre; or, The Ambiguities*, he describes the blank sheet of paper on which his hero is struggling to write: "If man must wrestle, perhaps it is well that it should be on the nakedest possible plain." The nakedest possible plain is a plain old sheet of paper.

During the winter, Melville used to begin his days, before striking out for the nakedest possible plain, by feeding a pumpkin to his cow. As the cow began to ruminate, so did he. No doubt he was grateful that she blessed his silence and aloneness and absurdity.

—Now go and write, she said to him after a few mouthfuls of pumpkin. I'll see you at four.

Yet there is a different sort of loneliness and perhaps a more vulgar form of sadness. I went walking on a beautiful afternoon after a fight with a friend, a quarrelsome back-and-forth over the telephone. I should have been happy with my own company after hanging up, since togetherness with her seemed a lost cause. I walked up to Edward's Heights, where I have walked a thousand times, always with a sense of exhilaration. Yet on this day the Heights did not elevate me: nature smiled, but I scowled. Halfway up the hill I turned back, disheartened, toward the cabin. What did I do when I got there? I don't remember. Probably I slumped and slouched, grumbled and groused, then hummed the Jagger classic "Paint It Black."

All the brisk talk we hear about "snapping out of it," "pulling yourself together," and whatever other proverbs and clichés rush to our rescue, rest on a misunderstanding. A mood cannot be chased away at will. Only one mood can replace another, says moody Martin Heidegger, and he's right. He's also right to say that moods color our perception of the entire world: when we are in the dumps, the world is dumpy, and everyone and everything in the world isn't so hot either. In other words, a mood attunes us to the world and tunes up that world always in a particular way. We tune in and pick up on the one frequency that is frequenting us. The rest goes flying past our ears. When I'm on top of the world, I can't even hear the laments of those in the dumps. Yesterday, when I was in the dumps, I could only take potshots at those ninnies who were cavorting on top of the world.

We have to hate this doctrine; we wish we could refute it. Yet refutation is hopeless. We will never find ourselves in the attunement or mood that would enable us to tune out of moods altogether. That's what the Stoics and Transcendentalists and wizards of all the ages and of all cultures have tried to get us to do. Delusions of mastery. Delusions arising from resentment toward the emotions. All we can do is keep a stiff upper lip, pull ourselves together, and stick with other such brave and dimwitted clichés that don't help. Almost anything can compel a simple and brave—and struggling—human being to sadness.

62

The work of mourning

Thoreau says he went into the woods to "conduct some private business," and readers assume he means the writing of *Walden*. Yet our editor corrects that assumption and assures us that the "private business" in question was the mourning of his dead brother John, with whom Henry had been close. Until recently they had directed a school together. Yet brother John was more than a professional partner: Emerson records the brothers once boarding a boat "which they have built with their own hands, with sails which they have contrived to serve as a tent by night, and [going] up the Merrimack to live by their wits on the fish of the stream and the berries of the wood" (J 151–52). No matter how close they may have been, however, the "private business" of Henry's mourning remains private. In all of *Walden*, nary a word about brother John's demise; the editor alone raises the veil on the silent mourner. Is this discretion on Thoreau's part? Is this the best or the worst of American Puritanism? Nowadays, when public confession is the newest circus in town and all the world's a *True Confessions* tabloid, where the mass of human beings lead lives of whining desperation, one wishes that more people could be like him, so that at least something of the private realm could be salvaged. Yet doesn't a writer have to try to disclose what is on his or her mind? Where do discretion and candor cross swords?

Perhaps Thoreau does provide a glimpse or two of his mourning—for example, in the following passage from "Where I Lived, and What I Lived For":

> I went to the woods because I wished to live deliberately, to front only the essential facts of life, and see if I could not learn what it had to teach, and not, when I came to die, discover that I had not lived. I did not wish to live what was not life, living is so dear; nor did I wish to practise resignation, unless it was quite necessary. I wanted to live deep and suck out all the marrow of life, to live so sturdily and Spartan-like as to put to rout all that was not life, to cut a broad swath and shave close, to drive life into a corner, and reduce it to its lowest terms, and, if it proved to be mean, why then to get the whole and genuine

meanness of it, and publish its meanness to the world; or if it were sublime, to know it by experience, and be able to give a true account of it in my next excursion. (W 67)

Living is so dear, whether *dear* means too costly or altogether worthy of love. In either case, one does not want to be resigned to the negative, one does not want to surrender too readily to death, unless and until capitulation is quite necessary, unless and until life, cornered like a hack politician and reduced to the lowest common denominator, proves nasty. Thoreau is interested in the meanness, not the meaning, of life. "Mean" in the sense of shabby and ungenerous. (Schopenhauer says that life is a business that doesn't cover its costs; Heidegger replies that life doesn't cover its costs because it is not a business.) Or, Thoreau continues, to see if life is sublime. True, the pleasure of the sublime, according to Immanuel Kant, is a negative pleasure; there is a grandeur that hurts even as we are called to salute it. The meanness *and* sublimity of dear life? Thoreau is perhaps struggling to regain and to acknowledge the *tragic* sense of life, which our civilization has lost.

Yet not to utter a single word about this brother, to encrypt him in silence and to inscribe no plaque or stone, not a single memorial or mention, seems odd. It seems disingenuous, to say the least, to leave the dead unmentioned and unmourned so that nobody will notice that brave chanticleer is missing a leg, that he hobbles as he crows. What does a "true account" of life require? What should Vigilante Hank be on the lookout for, and what should he be bringing to our attention, even at the risk of indiscretion? It isn't that death and mourning ought to prevail in his text or that his work should be all gloom and doom. It is merely that chanticleer should not be an ostrich.

63

A cautionary note

We know from the biographies of Henry that he was so affected by John's demise in 1842 (from lockjaw) that he suffered something like a nervous collapse. There are even suggestions that he was plagued by a mimetic repetition of John's illness by way of hysteric symptoms—which would account for the silence. Knowing that should give us pause. Who can prescribe how the work of mourning should go or what it may demand of us? Who can say whether the work of mourning is ever successful, or what such "success" could even mean? Who can say whether Henry's silence is something he himself has chosen? Perhaps that silence was inflicted on him? Sometimes one must submit to the ostrich in oneself to know the dark of the underworld.

Hurry up, please, it's time

A friend of mine died recently, quite unexpectedly, of mysterious causes. The doctors spoke of "sudden death syndrome," as though he were an infant. He had been enjoying a very productive period, publishing book after book, and very good books they were. A kind of conspiracy theory clouded my mind from the moment I received the news of his death: I said to myself that he had been in a hurry to get these things off his writing table, that he had sensed that the end was nigh. No one ever *knows*, of course; of that we may feel certain. What we mean when we give voice to this theory is that something in him was driving him to finish his work, even if death invariably leaves our projects and our selves equally unfinished—done, but unfinished—forever. Should that not make us stop short when friends of ours flatter us by saying how productive we have been in recent months or years? Are they not also saying something else under their breath as an aside?

—Better move at an even faster pace, my friend! All this productivity means that the disaster that has been biding its time is now crowding close.

How lucky for us that the conspiracy theory of productivity and death is simply a myth—a seductive yet wholly unfounded belief, the usual paranoia about the time of our lives. Yet what *is* the time of our lives? It is a time that at some point is irremediably "up."

65

Return to sender

Some years back I mailed condolences to the children of an aunt of mine who had just died. I did not know that the children, now grown, had in the meantime moved. The letter made its painstaking way back from the United States to Germany marked RTS (return to sender) even though my aunt's children may have moved but one block down the street. Life and death mean nothing now in our American neighborhoods—there is so much mobility, and so much isolation and alienation. Someone dies and the current occupant yawns and scribbles RTS. Thoreau's contemporaries, if not he himself, might have found "return to sender" a plausible description of death itself.

Former inhabitants, Part Three

The image of the Oma on the farm where I first lived in the Black Forest I will never forget. She was bending over a stuck pig, capturing its blood in a yellow plastic bucket. She then mixed milk into the blood, stirring the bubbly rose-colored elixir with her hand so that the blood would not coagulate and the milk not curdle. My own blood curdled at the sight, but the Oma could do lots of things at slaughtering time that I could never do. One would like to think that I had quasi-ethical reasons for being unable to do them. They were actually queasy-ethical reasons. When she asked me to fetch a bucket of water from the trough, my knees buckled. Yet fetch it I did, over and over again, inasmuch as the spilling of blood needs countless bucketsful of water—lustral, purgative water—to wash out the damned spot. However, the Oma was remarkable not only at pig-slaughtering time. When the Opa died in the night and I went the next morning to offer her my condolences, she spoke before I could.

—Nothing to be done. That's the way it is with human beings.

A snippet on schnapps

There are many varieties—purple or yellow plum, sour or sweet cherry, raspberry, apple-and-pear, Gentian root—but my favorite is *Hefeschnaps*, wine yeast schnapps, otherwise known as essence-of-the-purple-sludge-at-the-bottom-of-wine-barrels, or elixir-of-dregs, since it is blessed with many names. It is made from the lavender muck that sediments at the bottom of the wine barrel. The muck is gathered and brought to a boil and its fumes distilled; the cooled liquor is then cut by an equal amount of purified water. If it were not cut, the schnapps would be 200 proof, which is double the proof that even the most skeptical drinker needs. I have tasted this uncut, ur-schnapps, tasted it very gingerly: it closes the epiglottis, prevents air from entering the trachea, and so grants a preview of death by asphyxiation. Once thinned, however, *Hefeschnaps* is pure medicine. It is an all-purpose antiseptic for external and internal use, because it is free of prussic acid and is cleansing and soothing. It also functions, as I noted earlier, as central heating in winter. One might think that a schnapps made from the sludge at the bottom of a wine barrel would be the essence of sludge. It is instead the essence of essence. Every Transcendentalist needs a liter of it in the larder if he or she means to survive the winter.

Tell Marlonbrando your dreams, honey, and everything will be all right, Part Four

—My most horrible "task dream" is about the tiny shards of green glass I have to pick out of the gravel.

—Try to focus. Start at the beginning.

—It's Danteësque, nay, Kafkaesque. I don't want to talk about it.

—Good. Go on.

—There is a party in full swing. It is being held outside—on the gravel driveway of the house where I grew up, the same house that had the adobe wall, the house of the Bloomberry bush. I am the host. I have to arrange a million things. All I can remember is dashing from task to task, doing my best. I serve the wine in my best glass goblets, pale green *Römer* from Germany. Two young guests, I don't know who they are, they must be Russians, toast one another, drain their *Römer*, then smash the goblets on the ground. A million splinters of emerald glass disappear among the bits of gravel. I have to get down on all four and retrieve each piece. A woman stands over me scolding. I tell her I am doing my best. She snarls that my best is not good enough.

Marlonbrando is unimpressed by my harrowing "task dream." He seems bored with his own task, which is listening to me. Bored, or at least blasé, he begins to look more and more Gallic, as though his home were across the Rhine. He grins a Frenchified grin, more like a sneer, and rubs a digit pad of his paw against the thumb pad, as we do when we talk of money.

—Forty-five minutes, he says. *Avez-vous quelque chose pour moi, monsieur?* Have you a tidbit for me, my good man?

Doubling up

In his chapter on "Solitude," Thoreau develops a remarkable account of *thinking*, which he likens to a kind of *theater*. Herewith one of my favorite passages in all of *Walden*:

> With thinking we may be beside ourselves in a sane sense. By a conscious effort of the mind we can stand aloof from actions and their consequences; and all things, good and bad, go by us like a torrent. We are not wholly involved in Nature. I may be either the driftwood in the stream, or Indra in the sky looking down on it. I *may* be affected by a theatrical exhibition; on the other hand, I *may not* be affected by an actual event which appears to concern me much more. I only know myself as a human entity; the scene, so to speak, of thoughts and affections; and am sensible of a certain doubleness by which I can stand as remote from myself as from another. However intense my experience, I am conscious of the presence and criticism of a part of me, which, as it were, is not a part of me, but spectator, sharing no experience, but taking note of it; and that is no more I than it is you. When the play, it may be the tragedy, of life is over, the spectator goes his way. It was a kind of fiction, a work of the imagination only, so far as he was concerned. This doubleness may easily make us poor neighbors and friends sometimes. (W 101)

What Emerson took to be aloofness and perhaps even abrasiveness Thoreau here attributes to the duplicity of human thinking and existence, a duplicity or tendency to doubling that the text demonstrates when Thoreau first invokes "a theatrical exhibition" as the opposite of the real then indicates that we are all really "spectators" at the very real "play of life." Such doubleness or duplicity makes us friends and neighbors sometimes only by half. The other half observes—with varying degrees of involvement and distance—the tragic spectacle. Why tragic? Perhaps because in it one can lose a brother.

Perhaps also because one can also *observe oneself* losing a brother, as though losing twice over, again with shifting degrees of involvement and distance.

Plato defined thinking as the silent dialogue of the soul with itself, which a more modern idiom would define as talking to yourself . . . quietly, so they don't cart you off. Before Plato, Empedocles began one of his great poems by saying δίπλ᾽ ἐρέω, "A twofold tale I shall tell," or "I shall speak of doublings," or perhaps "I shall speak duplicitously, with forked tongue, as it were." We have all experienced the dialogue of self and soul, I suppose, often in those secret thoughts we entertain behind the thoughts we publicize. There are so many levels in and of consciousness—the word *doubling* hardly does them justice. We may even experience this redoubled splintering or multilayering of consciousness when we seem to be most at one with ourselves and with one another. When I am beneath my lover, watching her smile, feeling her breasts draw faint lines on my chest with their soft penmanship, I am lost to multiplicity, it seems, and am utterly at one with her. But no. It is precisely in this moment of union that each of us shivers into manifold surfaces. I watch her, and I watch her watching my watching her watching me watch her, and she does the same, although of course entirely differently. And it is much more than heavenly spectation. The two of us are there together; yet each of the two reverberates singly. Our entirely separate childhoods and adulthoods entwine here, behind the scenes and in the wings, as it were; the metaphor of the theater goes backstage, where much goes on that we are not able to watch, not ever. We have to dissolve into our own singularized batch of multiple selves, or else we are not there for one another at all. I do see who I am with, and grateful to be with, yet I see now without looking, no longer watching, and it speaks to me in my head, albeit not in so many words.

—What an extraordinary person she is—all of her! How lucky you are—all of you!

The *you* in this case refers to *me*, which is to say, to one or several of the selves that I am—and, if I am very fortunate, to all of them. In any case, deepest in, I am farthest out, electrifyingly aware of both the intimacy and the remoteness. Intimacy is eccentric, elliptical and hyperbolic at once. This is what Robert Musil's Ulrich and Agathe learn after fifteen hundred pages of trying to become *one*. (Musil's first name for Ulrich was *Anders*, which in German means "otherwise.") But to return to Thoreau's theater of thinking.

The spectator at a play, perhaps a tragedy, is hardly indifferent to what is going on down there on the stage: it is Richard Burton doing *Hamlet*

132

or Dustin Hoffman doing Willy Loman or Irene Pappas doing *Medea*, and I am more than interested—I am captivated, totally absorbed. Yet even in this total absorption there is a part of me that, as Thoreau says, "remains aloof" or at least aloft.

—What a great play—and it *is* a play! What a great performance—and it *is* a performance! She is *acting* down there! And she is convincing me utterly!

The critical instance of which Thoreau speaks is not the result of a callous cut. Yet criticism—the "cut" or "split" that the word *crisis* (κρίσις) implies—is always there, even and especially in the moments of greatest absorption. The great German poet and theoretician of the theater Friedrich Hölderlin called such a moment the *caesura*, borrowing the word from poetics, where it means an interruption in the rhythm or flow of a line, caused perhaps by a mere mark of punctuation. Hölderlin thought of the tragic play as a rhythmic sequence of scenes rushing toward a conclusion and therefore needing to be slowed down; sometimes the beginning of a play has to be protected by this *caesura*, or "counterrhythmic interruption," inserted early on (*Oedipus the Tyrant* is like that, he says), whereas sometimes it is the end that needs rescue and deceleration (*Antigone* is like that, he adds). The odd thing that happens during the interruption and the slowdown is that the spectator manages to catch a glimpse of the play as a whole, what it is about and what it is for, and so in that instant he or she sees the embodied dramatic representation *as* a representation. Ironically, it is at this very moment of doubling, or redoubling—the very moment when we see the play for what it is, a play—that we are most moved by it. No, not merely moved, but seized, snatched up and torn away from the midpoint of our lives, removed to what Hölderlin calls the "ex-centric realm of the dead." A great play knocks us silly, and the blow of clarity comes at the moment of *caesura*. In that moment, we are completely absorbed by Medea's or Willy Loman's fate, and yet we can see and cite particular details.

—I can't believe what Dustin Hoffman just did! Did you see that gesture? Where did he get the idea to do that?!

In other words, the doubling and multilayering, the shivering or splintering of consciousness does not have to imply a loss of intensity, focus, commitment, or engagement. We are like kids again, playing a game: that little game is the most important thing in the world right now, perhaps the only thing. The effect of the play on us—what Aristotle calls *catharsis*, by which he means the refinement, distillation, and intensification of the feelings of terror and compassion in us, leading to the ultimate release of

133

all such intense feelings—depends on this counterrhythmic interruption in the sequence of scenes. We get worked on and worked over emotionally all the more intensely as our critical instance takes distance.

—Look, it's just a play!

And our heart replies,

—But what a play! I didn't think anyone knew us this well!

The critic then joins the grand conspiracy of the drama and helps it work. Sometimes, all our selves seem to join hands and form a common front, so that the play—perhaps it is the play of life itself, Thoreau says—cannot be resisted. We are not poorer friends for that, but richer, especially when we are the fortunate flesh that is destined for soft penmanship.

Thoreau's editor notes that Henry "was never able to lose himself completely in any emotion," and he calls this "an interesting psychological problem" (W 288n. 11). It is. Yet it is also far more than a problem. For every disciple of Dionysos is double—think of Nietzsche, not the simplest and not the least critical of men. Perhaps even the Maenads in their dance across the winter snows of Parnassos are *thinking*, thinking within the *theater* in which they are so entirely caught up.

—The things the god asks us to do! My poor feet!

Thinking and every kind of theory are captivated by theater. And theater is sometimes comic, sometimes tragic, sometimes tragicomic, doubling up with laughter and convulsion and critical consciousness by turns.

My little chickadee!

At exactly ten minutes past three in the afternoon of the first of April (no fooling!) a chickadee, looking to build a home, entered the birdhouse affixed to the east wall of the cabin. I had been awaiting this moment for weeks, fearful that it would never come—on account of Marlonbrando. Yet the cat ate early today and has made himself scarce ever since. The chickadee sat at the entrance and stuck her head in the front door—I assume an important job like this has to be done by the she-bird—and lifted her ice-cream spoon tail as her head dipped down inside the house. Her partner was up in the boughs of Douglas the Fir, checking out the 'hood. She flew up to join him, they discussed the pros and cons a while and whether they could afford it; they flitted about, and then she returned and dropped in. I now saw her tiny head looking out the front door (the only door) of the

house at me. What a thrill! I am a chickadee landlord! But soft! For the past ten minutes there's been no activity around the house. Who knows what the finicky couple has decided? Real estate is a nerve-racking business. A landlord's life is hard, no one understands our tribulations. Just in case the deal goes through, however, I'm going to move Marlonbrando's bowl and water cup around to the front of the cabin. My visitors are so few that I can't afford to have them savoring one another.

Home Entertainment Center

Just now I heard a cuckoo, and I wasn't in the woods. Last night, I wasn't on the meadow and still I heard a lark. In both cases, the windows of the cabin were shut tight. The cuckoo was brought to me by Beethoven's Sixth, the lark by Richard Strauss's fourth and last of the "Four Last Songs." I wonder if the greatest single difference between Thoreau's and "my" cabins isn't the CD player I acquired several Christmases ago. I now enjoy Baroque mornings and Romantic evenings, intermezzoed by absolutely Classical afternoons. The one sadness of spring and summer is that I work and eat outside, where Mahler is forced to retire his frenzied baton.

In earlier days, before I would leave the States for the cabin, I'd have to make the most important decision of the whole trip: I selected the CDs I would then slip into a portable canvas carrier. More fateful still, I had to leave a whole discotheque of friends behind—the red priest of Venice; the balding, brooding Sibelius; provocative Prokofiev; and the artful Saint-Saëns. Now, in retirement, they are all with me.

What more can I say? The terrible thing about music is that no one can say anything about it without sounding like liner notes. The choices appear to be two: (1) write so technically that no one can follow you or (2) be so sublime and lyrical that no one wants to follow you. One yearns to express gratitude for the music, but every sincere asseveration and every sigh of praise is an insult to musical experience. Even Nietzsche regretted most of what he had written about music in *The Birth of Tragedy*. Schelling has an unforgettable passage in the first draft of his *Ages of the World*: he says that when the Great Goddess roars by in her chariot—the goddess to whom men must sacrifice their most prized possessions—the wheels of her chariot, rimmed with copper, sing out. The tumult of copper on cobblestone is the origin of music, he says, and music the origin of tragedy. It sort of makes you afraid to turn on the Home Entertainment Center.

72

Neighbors, Part Five: Rüdiger

Rüdiger gets more and more discouraged with each passing year. The US-American company he used to work for (installing and repairing beer and soft drink vending machines) had grown more and more brutal as cheap labor became increasingly available in Germany and jobs increasingly scarce. So Rüdiger started his own firm, with himself the sole worker. The politicians here in Germany talk big about helping the common man, says Rüdiger, and they pocket uncommonly large sums of the money the common man earns. The politicians in the United States talk bigger about helping the common man and pocket larger sums of money, he adds, if only in the form of a question to me. Rüdiger is not sure that Americanization is an improvement. Things are also difficult closer to home, however, right here in the village. Thieves have begun to snitch the antique wooden statues from the nativity scene in the church at Christmas time; they have also started to steal the solar energy panels from the rooftops of houses and barns. Rüdiger has now wired his solar installation with solar electricity, so that if a thief latches onto the panel he may never let go but form a lasting attachment. I will suggest to Rüdiger that we wire Saint Joseph the same way. One should embrace the saints, but cautiously.

Rüdiger is in his early fifties, and he agrees that he is overweight. That is what the doctors in the city tell him, and doctors are honorable men and women. Yet Rüdiger is large because, come summer, he lifts entire haystacks and carries them over his shoulder to the hay wagon. The only person I have seen push him around is Anton the Goat. But Anton pushes everyone around. Rüdiger makes no claims about being able to repair the broken world. Yet when something goes on the blink in the cabin—the water pump, a faucet, an electric socket—he is right there with his toolkit. If a repair doesn't go well, he smacks the offending part with a wrench. He sees me jump whenever he does this, and so he explains this maneuver with a smile.

—Everything works better with a bit of gentle violence, he says.

The forlorn pair of shoes

What astute engineer designed the Black Forest cow stall? I do not know. Sing his or her praises I must. The floor is designed in such a way that when the cows do Number One (that is what we city boys used to call it) it flows directly into a trench in the concrete. The floor is constructed at a delicate angle off the horizontal, perhaps only one or two degrees, so that the Number One flows—majestically, mississippily—toward a grill at the end of the trench. It trickles through the grill, leaving behind whatever coarser matter, whether straw or worse, may have accompanied it, down to a vast metal container underneath the stall floor. There it sits through fall and winter, aging and ripening like the choicest of wines until early spring, at which point the farmer pumps the bovine Number One into a portable tank that he has attached to the back of his Bulldog. (Do not alert the SPCA: *Bulldog* is the generic German name for a tractor—because of the insignia on the Mack truck and/or tractor, Mack being once upon a time the most prolific manufacturer of farm vehicles in Germany.) From thence the aged, nitrogen-rich Number One is driven out onto the meadow in March and sprayed in a vast, aromatic, milk-chocolaty arc over the dormant grasses.

And here is how I helped. The transfer from the stall's subterranean tank to the portable tank attached to the Bulldog entails a delicate procedure and sometimes requires extra hands. And feet. The farmer had his Bulldog out on the street, which was the only spot available for it. The makeshift hose that ran from the subterranean vault to the portable tank had several sections to it—sections, segments, extensions, call them what you will. I was asked to grip the splice in the hose right in the middle of the road, just before the nitrogen-rich elixir flowed into the portable tank. Did I falter? I did not.

I was wearing a pair of shoes that I never really liked. (This seems off the topic, but it is very much on, you already know that.) They had been cheap, and after I bought them, I understood why. Inside they were lined with artificial leather, *escaille* I think they call it, a kind of plastic that doesn't breathe and that eventually cracks and irritates the foot. The only way you can tell it is *escaille* and not true leather is that *escaille* has no fragrance, whereas genuine leather has that deep, sweet, life-giving smell comparable only to coffee in the morning. Or a bakery. If there is no bakery and no coffee shop in your vicinity, look for a handbag boutique. Honestly. It will get you through the day, unless, understandably, skins are a thing you have forbidden yourself.

The problem with those cheap shoes of mine—they were brown, I remember, and they were never in style, so that they could never be out of it—was that they had no character, no dignity, no atmosphere of the living. That was about to change. About that hose splice . . . Ah, attentive reader, you surmised it long ago: either it or I did not hold.

I left those shoes out on the terrace for a year of seasons. Neither rain nor snow nor hail nor sleet nor lilac in the dooryard blooming had the slightest impact on those shoes. A year after that fatal, fetid day, I marched with them—not on my feet but in my outstretched hands—out to the garbage bin, chanting the sacred entry song in Gregorian. The next time the farmer asked me if I'd mind taking up my former post at the schizoid splice I told him that I no longer possessed the proper attire. He was disappointed in me. Like the cows, however, I felt a certain relief.

The forlorn BMW

As Rüdiger drove the portable cow pee wagon out onto the meadow, he felt the chill down to his bones. There are days in early spring as cold as anything winter has to offer. And sometimes the wind is up—as it was on that day. Rüdiger decided to commence the bovine benediction of the fields with the small triangular patch near the parking area, where the village street comes to an end. He drove the Bulldog carefully along the hypotenuse of the field and released the "spray" lever. When the wind came up—and it was a freezing wind out of the north, old Boreas himself—Rüdiger flipped his collar up and drove back and forth across the meadow, his eye fixed on the fine brown line forming on the field. When he had finished drenching the field, Rüdiger glanced to the south toward the parking area. Only one car was parked there, the car of an intrepid hiker who apparently did not mind the freezing temperature and the rude north wind. As far as Rüdiger could tell, it was a new model BMW, that is, a vehicle manufactured by the

Bayrische Motoren Werke according to specifications the company hoped would challenge and, yes, even surpass those of the Mercedes Benz. This particular BMW, on this particular day, had a mottled brown chassis. It also had mottled brown wheels and mottled brown windows.

Rüdiger gasped.

At that moment, the hiker returned from his walk. He stood frozen on the spot, as it were. Rüdiger waited for the cursing to begin, but all was silence, except for the relentless wind.

—Is that your car? Rüdiger asked shyly.

The stranger nodded slowly, said nothing.

—It's new, isn't it? Rüdiger remarked more than asked.

The stranger spoke now, in a hushed, crushed voice.

—I picked it up from the dealership last week.

Rüdiger said nothing further. An apology seemed somehow out of place. He began to think of the lawsuit that would destroy him and his family. He hoped that a northerly breeze was an act of God. These anxious thoughts were interrupted by a sight Rüdiger had never seen before. The stranger was crying. He stood before his formerly silver BMW with black leather interior and he wept.

It took them some time, working together, to get the door on the driver's side open. The mottled milk-chocolate crust had frozen it shut. The stranger drove off after Rüdiger managed to scrape the windshield clean. Well, not exactly clean: a sort of porthole in the otherwise solid wall of seasoned, frozen cow piss.

Weeks later Rüdiger learned that the dealership had replaced the car. A special task force had tried for many days to get the stench out of the leather interior. The silver exterior had come clean almost immediately, but the interior—in spite of the fact that the BMW is a wonderfully engineered automobile and its doors and windows seal tighter than a drum—resisted all the detergents and deodorizing agents known to man.

It was just like my shoes, except that the seats were real leather, and they smelled of cowhide. Earlier on, anyway. One of life's little ironies— bovine revenge, you might say.

Kids

Black and tawny goats, all young females some eight weeks old by now, romp in the springtime snow. They play Follow the Leader, Queen of the Hill, Cowgirl Skiing, and Billie Goat Gruff with one another. They perform a ballet leap or two, steering clear of their cranky mothers, who want them off the teat. Sometimes the little ones get confused and play Hump the Hostess. The hostess in this case is the smallest goat, the most recently born. She takes it all with amazing aplomb, accepting these misguided attentions from her older cousins and merely walking off when they get too carried away. They do not butt heads yet, though they will start doing so, I am told, as soon as their cranky mothers prevail and they are fully weaned. Girls will be girls, but for the moment, they are just kids.

Henry's mom and dad

Does he mention them anywhere? Certainly not in *Walden*. Our editor tells us that his mother and sister paid his bills and his taxes while he was away at Walden Pond and that his poll tax was surreptitiously paid by an aunt. (He had refused to pay it as an act of resistance to slavery and the Mexican War and was arrested for that refusal.) None of these women are mentioned, nor is papa. Maybe Henry himself was Homunculus, the miniature spirit seed of humankind, born in a bottle—one of Goethe's most hilarious parables in *Faust II*, and his wisest. However, whereas Homunculus is carried off to the Ionian shores of ancient Greece in search of a body, having grown weary of bumping his soul against the glass, Hank the Homunc flies off in search of a soul, a soul that will ratiocinate and refrigerate. "Ice is an interesting subject for contemplation. . . . It is commonly said that this is the difference between the affections and the intellect" (W 224). That is why mom and dad are missing. They are being kept on ice, inasmuch as parents both effect and affect us, and the feelings surrounding them most often overwhelm us, even if we account ourselves clever.

More work of mourning

It is meet and just to criticize Thoreau for neglecting the theme of mourning—that "private business" that brought him to Walden Pond in the first place. Meet and just and self-righteous and shortsighted. Last night, I received a phone call from my son telling me of the death of a friend's father, a man I had met and admired. As I thought about this universal passing of human beings, about this mortality that, philosophically considered, is the single most important aspect of human being (with the possible exceptions of sexuality, gestation, and birth, which are also rites of passing), the aspect we share with everything that lives, I looked at the day's date on the face of my wristwatch. I saw that it was the anniversary of my own mother's death. I had been anticipating this date for weeks, especially after the anniversary—sixteen days earlier—of my father's death, so that there was no explanation for my having forgotten it. None, as Marlonbrando would insist, except for the supernatural power of repression, or "active forgetfulness," as Nietzsche calls it. It took another man's death to bring me back to my own, that is, to my mother's passing and my own death.

I touched her hand. The skin had turned to parchment.

The stretch of life that takes us from the silky breast to the silk lining of the coffin is unimaginable. When we see the vast arc of a long life—but always from a confined perspective, always within our own narrow world—the overwhelming vision makes us just about faint. We haven't the strength for it. Perhaps it is the inconceivable expenditure of energy that must go into any given life—again, the *exertion* of life—that so overwhelms us: the energy of mothers and fathers, teachers and friends, lovers and companions. These combined synergies augment the energy of each living person dedicated to this or that project, this or that passion, this or that folly. William Butler Yeats, in "Among School Children," first taught me about this expenditure of energy—or, rather, first put into words what I had always known in some inchoate way even as a boy.

I had touched her hand often in life, both when I was a boy and when she was an old woman sitting in her favorite chair through the night because she was afraid to lie down, the breathing came so hard. Her skin was not parchment then.

We had attended a funeral together, she and I, early on in my life—a kindergarten classmate whose name I never knew. The child, having done something unforgivably naughty, threw himself off the roof of his house. I remember thinking that he must have been testing the Superman hypothesis. Yet my mother, holding my hand tight as we walked home from the funeral parlor, spoke to me in a subdued tone of voice.

—No matter what you ever do, no matter how bad you feel about what you've done, you must never hurt yourself. Promise me.

I had no idea what she was talking about. I promised.

Now that I have done a few naughty things in the eyes of the world and even in my own eyes, I understand better. I waited until her eyes were closed forever to do the thing she would have found most deplorable. One of the terrible secrets of human life is that every death, even the most mourned, is also a liberation. After Alfred's horrendously procrastinated and painful passing, Enid announces that there are some changes impending, some long-delayed *Corrections* to be made. Comedy can be as harsh as tragedy.

One of the most astonishing ideas I have heard in my life is that there is some measure of mourning involved in every experience of the beautiful. It is an idea developed by the French philosopher Jacques Derrida. He says somewhere that beauty, far from being eternal, always betrays its transience, its passing, so that when we see a beautiful thing or person—a painting or a landscape or a lover—we always have the thought (spoken as an aside in the drama of our life) that it or he or she will not last, that some terrible vulnerability or fragility alone holds us together. For the time being.

The claims that love conquers death and that beauty is immortal are crass and insulting. Only the realization that love and beauty will pass into oblivion, into the unmarked grave of the past, grants them their awful power. Eternity everlasting is the time of the grotesque and the resentful. Aesthetics is the science of bereavement.

A few moments ago I checked my answering machine and heard the voice of my daughter Elena, a voice I have not heard for months. It was piping, breathless, youthful, and confused.

—I guess you're out walking somewhere . . .

I did not delete the message, hoping to preserve that tremulous voice for all time. Prayer, I suppose, was invented by parents who needed to be assured that they would die before their offspring. My mother was a great one for prayer. I used to look up at her in church with the realization that she was inscrutable also in that respect. I tried to move my lips with that automatic ease of devotion, but it never worked, even though I did see how beautiful she was.

Tell Marlonbrando your dreams, honey, and everything will be all right, Part Five

—I call it "the ambulance dream." It contains the best and the worst of my dreams.

Marlonbrando flicks his tail, smiles his distant smile, the smile that keeps its secrets.

—A tale of two cities, he says. Go on.

—I need to give you some background. What I'll tell you now is real, not the dream.

—Real? says Marlonbrando dreamily. Go on.

—During my early teenage years, my father had to have surgery. He was now at home recuperating. We children were lying on the floor one evening watching TV when we heard my father cry out in terror from the bedroom. His incision had burst open.

—Where was the incision? What kind of surgery was it?

—Across the abdomen. Hernia. His fifth or sixth operation in the same place. The repairs never lasted, the wire they used only shredded the muscle tissue. And now not even the stitches held.

—Surgery has made progress since then.

—I'll never forget the smell: acrid antiseptic mixed with the putrefaction of infection. He was bleeding. The bedsheet was shockingly red. We pressed a towel over the wound and called an ambulance.

—Don't tell me how long it took for the ambulance to get there . . .

—When we were finally on our way to the hospital, I found myself—for reasons I never understood—in the back of the ambulance with my father. My mother was up front next to the driver.

—That's odd. . . . What did you do during the trip?

—I held his hand, for the first time in my life.

—You'd never held hands before?

—He had always held my hand. Now I was holding his. Very different.

—Go on.

—As the ambulance made its way to the hospital—about a half-hour ride—I reported our progress to my father: turning left onto Beck's Run

Road, passing Madeline Avenue and then the waterworks, where another kindergarten classmate of mine drowned . . .

—It's a wonder any of you survived kindergarten.

—. . . speeding down the four-lane highway to Carson Street. The siren was intermittent until we got into the city. Left on Carson Street into the South Side of town and, at last, the emergency entrance of the hospital on the right.

—Did he recover?

—He did. The new repair held.

—So why are you telling me this?

—Because my father later told me that my reporting the ambulance's progress had been a great comfort to him, that it had eased his fright.

—You felt proud?

—No, not proud. I felt love.

—His of you or yours of him?

—Both. Both ways. Maybe for the first time.

Marlonbrando sees that I am having trouble with my eyes. He waits for the trouble to pass. He is a fellow animal, after all.

—And all of this is taken up into your dream?

—For ten years after his death, I dreamt the "ambulance dream" repeatedly, until finally it became less frequent and then ceased altogether.

—Did you have other dreams of him—nightmares, perhaps?

—The ambulance dream dispelled all the nightmares before they could start.

—Tell me the dream.

—It begins in the ambulance. We are speeding past Madeline Avenue, the waterworks, down the four-lane highway to Carson Street. This time, though, my dad is in greater distress: it isn't a burst incision but a heart attack. That's how he died years later. Heart attack.

—His distress must be your own.

—It is. Terrible. Yet in the dream my father, seeing or sensing my terror, sits up on the stretcher and takes my hand. His expression and his voice are quiet and reassuring. "It's all right, it's all right," he says, "I'm already dead."

—"I am already dead." Spoken reassuringly?

—He was an engineer. His heart attack began while he was laboring over blueprints. He was checking someone else's blueprints to make sure they were error free. That's what he did. He reassured.

—And now in the dream he was helping you with your mourning. Soberly, like an engineer.

—Soberly. Symmetrically.

—In spite of the fact that the walls are never four-square, the lines never perfectly plumb.

—I would always awaken from the dream at the precise moment he informed me that he was already dead. Yet it wasn't those words that stayed in my mind as I crossed the threshold to wakefulness. What lingered after the dream were the words, "It's all right."

Marlonbrando speaks slowly now, so softly that I do not hear him. But I know what he is saying in my own head.

—Words of release. No further task. Nothing to be done.

Old people

"I have lived some thirty years on this planet, and I have yet to hear the first syllable of valuable or even earnest advice from my seniors. They have told me nothing, and probably cannot tell me any thing, to the purpose" (W 5–6). Thoreau's contempt for the elderly is as American as retirement villages and bingo. Even the more pious Emerson shares Thoreau's contempt for the old: "What an obstinate illusion is that which in youth gives respect to the old!" he exclaims (J 403). Filial piety counts for little or nothing stateside. When they hit Los Angeles, Aeneas will finally shake Anchises off his back.

I remember visiting the home of a high school chum whose grandmother spoke no English. She jabbered at us in some foreign tongue.

—What is she saying? I asked my friend.

—It doesn't matter, he replied with a laugh. She's senile.

I was shocked to hear him say the word in her presence. Perhaps she *did* know some American words—and *senile* would have been among the very first words she would have understood, along with *Alzheimer's*.

Adoration of youth is common to most nations, but contempt for age seems to be a specifically US-American contribution to world culture. We are the proud bearers of the longest-standing metaphysical belief, to wit, that time is the enemy. Aristotle says that according to some philosophers time is the *origin* of all things, since all things *come to be* in time. Yet those are more correct, he says, who see time as the flood that sweeps everything into senescence, decrepitude, and death. We love youthful life and we hate liver spots, which do not augur well for the future. At all events, Henry is adamant about the old folks. Seniors beware!

> What old people say you cannot do you try and find that you can. Old deeds for old people, and new deeds for new. Old people did not know enough once, perchance, to fetch fresh fuel to keep the fire a-going; new people put a little dry wood under a pot, and are whirled round the globe with the speed of birds, in a way to kill old people, as the phrase is. Age is not better, hardly so well, qualified for an instructor as youth, for it has not profited so much as it has lost. One may almost

doubt if the wisest man has learned any thing of absolute value by living. Practically, the old have no very important advice to give the young, their own experience has been so partial, and their lives have been such miserable failures, for private reasons, as they must believe; and it may be that they have some faith left which belies that experience, and they are only less young than they were. (W 5)

My own experience of the elderly is so different from Thoreau's that it is doubtless un-American. Not only now that I am old, listing toward wrinkle and liver spot, but also when I was very young and rebellious, the elderly were either potentially or actually wise, and if they were fools, they had to prove it to me. Very few of them did so.

Here in the village, age is worn with pride, although without delusions of grandeur. The persons in Sankt Ulrich whom I knew and admired when I and they were younger have become even more worthy of respect. The forester who first taught me the trees forty years ago no longer works in the forest, but I like nothing better than accompanying him on walks there and learning still more from him. He teaches me something new and useful about wood and the woods each time we are together. Not by gabbing: he was slow to speak back then, and he is slower now; he smiles more and takes a little more time to explain, as though by growing older he had more time, not less, and more to smile about. True, during the hay harvest he is a four-star general commanding the Bulldog Armored Division, and you'd better not get in his way. Yet most of the time he'll take time to chat. For example, after repairing my axe. And even if his remarks sometimes seem odd, they carry authority.

The other morning, after I had fetched my milk at Frau K.'s, our paths crossed when he emerged from the barn. A blackbird, perched in the crown of a giant larch, was singing its heart and throat out. I gestured toward the bird.

—Does it sing like that every morning?

—Every morning and every evening.

The forester paused and looked over his shoulder, making certain no one was there to overhear.

—We have a bird feeder out on the terrace. He is thanking us for it. They do that.

I looked for a sign that he was joking, but his smile was not ironic, it was Franciscan. He has spent more than fifty years in the forest among the birds, the same birds that used to eat out of his father's hand. I knew the Opa, his father, and I believe that story about him too. It reminds me of a moment Thoreau reports with such tenderness that we wish he would always be like that—the Thoreau of thaw rather than of Thor. In "Winter Animals," he writes: "I once had a sparrow alight upon my shoulder for a moment while I was hoeing in a village garden, and I felt that I was more distinguished by that circumstance than I should have been by any epaulet I could have worn" (W 208).

The Opa died in his bed one bitter winter night. In his final hours, he was tended by a neighbor woman who had been a nurse during the war and who now ran her own small farm down the road. Darkness had long since descended. The Opa turned to her and spoke his last words:

—Frieda, go home, feed your cows.

It was on the following morning that the Oma explained to me how it was with human beings. And how nothing can be done about it.

Old people here know lots of very practical things. After having pitched hay up in the hayloft one August, I felt my lungs fill with fluid—a reaction to the chaff and dust. For a month, I visited doctors in Freiburg and swallowed pharmaceuticals. Nothing helped. A neighbor of the forester (we met her a moment or two ago: Frau S.M., who knows all the foodstuffs and all the weeds) heard my hacking cough and took me out into the pasture behind her house. She picked leaves from three sorts of plants.

—Dry these out over your *Kunsht*, not in the sunlight. Make a tea, drink three cups a day.

By the third day, the cough was gone. I very much wanted to believe that it was a coincidence or that the store-bought medicines were finally kicking in. After all, I am a child of the Enlightenment. Later I learned that what she had plucked for me were sprigs of wild thyme (*Thymus serpyllum L.*) and leaves of *Schafgarbe* and *Spitzwegerich* (*Achillea millefolium L.* and *Plantago lanceolata L.*), the ethereal oils of which were presumably present in all the medicines I'd been taking. For some reason, the tea or infusion worked, whereas the pills had not.

Old people here also know lots of very impractical things. The same forester who taught me the trees came to me one day to tell me that a Mozart mass was going to be played and sung in the monastery church at Sankt Ulrich that Sunday and that I should be sure to go. Frau K., who supplies me with a liter of fresh milk twice a week—unpasteurized, unhomogenized, unindustrialized—told my brother and me one Christmas Eve about the supremely impractical Mystery of the Barn. It is one of the ancient mysteries—Plato reports it in his dialogue called *Statesman*. Frau K. blushed a little as she related the mystery. My brother and I were eating a plaited yeast bread chock-full of almonds and raisins, washing it down with a large glass of local *Gutedel* wine and a small glass of local apple-and-pear schnapps. We were all aglow with Christmas, and Frau K. judged that we catechumens were ready to be baptized.

In a Schwarzwald *Hof*, or farmhouse, the animals and humans live under the same roof. A kind of mudroom behind the kitchen wall separates the family's living quarters from the stall, but if you press your ear against that wall, you can sometimes hear the animals.

—When we were children, she said, our parents would take us to that wall every Christmas Eve, toward midnight. We pressed up close . . . so that we could hear the animals talking.

—Talking?

—They talk only once a year. They pass on the news they've heard—of Jesus' birth. He was born in a stall, and their ancestors were there.

We all laughed. Her face was bright red, her eyes looking from side to side in embarrassment and anticipation. She then looked up to the clock on the wall.

—Ten o'clock. Two more hours.

It was clear to my brother and me that after all these years she was still going to the wall to hear the animals whisper the gospel. Plato's *Statesman* tells of an earlier epoch in human history, back before humans were forced to fend for themselves; it was a sort of Golden Age in which the gods and titans shepherded us. One of the most remarkable differences between the two epochs was that back then human beings could talk to the animals—and *listen* to them. We were a lot smarter back then, Plato says. Maybe that's how the old forester knew about the blackbird's thanksgiving, although he doesn't seem as old as all that. Maybe that's how Frau K. understood what was being communicated among the animals behind the wall.

Who knows but that old people might partake of old wisdoms from antique ages? Thoreau would scoff at this, I know, and I suppose he would be right. I too want to be on the side of youth and cleverness; I too want to be a true American. And yet. Old people—many of them, at least—help me out of the quandaries and quagmires of my enormous inexperience. And, like the other animals, they tell the best stories.

153

About that blackbird

The forester thinks it's singing out of gratitude to humans for the birdfeeder, but I know it is singing for sex. It perches in full view on the highest branches of larch or pine and sings the most variegated song, warbles like Homer, Dante, Shakespeare, and Paul McCartney rolled into one and supplied with sleek feathers. Last night, at dusk, the blackbird settled onto the top branch of a beech below the cabin and regaled me. I stood there for many minutes, unmoving yet moved. This morning, I walked through the forest to fetch my milk (today is Frau K.'s seventieth birthday, and I exchanged a bottle of Alsatian *Crémant* for a bottle of creamy milk), and I heard the insistent song of another kind of bird.

—Needyou! he cried.

—I need you too, I rejoined.

But I was lying. All I need is the blackbird (*die Amsel* in German), the polyglot of songbirds. Paul McCartney, yes, but also Freddie Mercury, Rufus Wainwright, Laurie Anderson, Dawn Upshaw, Elena Sophia, and Elias and Bob Dylan.

Incidentally, I love the way Thoreau, accepting a time-honored literary tradition, tries to transcribe birdsong and other animal speech acts into letters. The screech owls ululate like an ancient tragic chorus, *u-lu-lu*, or go twangy like a Nashville country-western tweetie bird, *Oh-o-o-o-o that I never had been bor-r-r-r-n!* The hoot owls trill an unlikely *hoorer hoo*, which is just a hoot, while the bullfrog delivers himself of an emphatic *tr-r-roonk!* I conjure up for myself a menagerie of sound and song, with foxes that grin slyly and go *hmmm!* and snakes that narrow their eyes and say *ssso-sssorry!* I want a horsefly that goes *zapbap!* a hedgehog that goes *waddlewaddlesnorflesniff!* and of course a cat that yells *stella! stella!* but most of all a blackbird who asserts his perch on larch or beech and trembles with a song that translates as *Hailtoyouladiesofthewoodcome-come-come-to-me!* Only when I possess all of these voluble animals will I be content.

Former inhabitants, Part Four:
The lover suspended in the rafters

What follows is the potentially true story of Anton Schaefer and Maria Magdalena Fromm. Anton was the shepherd of the Möhlin Valley in the Black Forest, Maria Magdalena the oldest daughter of the family that occupied the Bonnihof. On Christmas Eve, 1625, Anton looped a noose of hemp around his hirsute neck and, having secured the other end of the rope to the roofbeam of the Bonnihof cow stall, plunged into the gloom. He gave the rope his full weight; in return, the rope gave him two meters of freefall. It would be unreasonable to assume that he heard the snap, absurd to speculate that he felt the electric surge in his spine and loins.

Maria Magdalena Fromm's father had inherited the Bonnihof and so was something more than a simple peasant. In England, he would have been hailed as a yeoman, but dwelling here in the Black Forest, in the territory perpetually in dispute between the bishoprics of Staufen and Freiburg, he was simply the farmer who owed a greater weight of potatoes to the monastery than any other farmer in the valley. Helmbrecht Fromm had no sons. This was his tragedy, or at least the cruelest of cruel fates. For his oldest daughter, Maria Magdalena, would bring the next owner of the Hof under his own roof; his surname would be extinguished as soon as the couple exchanged their vows in the monastery church. Add to this the fact that his daughter was the most magnificent young woman of the valley, as of the many surrounding valleys north to Baden-Baden and east to the source of the Danube, and one gains a sense of the father's suffering. Like the first flower of spring, Maria Magdalena had already begun to draw swarms of buzzing hopefuls to the Bonnihof. Old men who were widowers, young men full of hope and ambition, masters and journeymen, local lords, and sons of great and small landowners—all responded to her chaste call, the call that she herself never made. Even the younger monks at the monastery allowed their eyes to linger too long on her, felt the prick of lust or longing beneath their habits and tasted the wickedness of delectation in their hearts: they no doubt prostrated themselves both at the altar of their salvation and in their unadorned cells, and only after the most desperate measures were they able to release the pressure of their sins. Helmbrecht Fromm kept a wary eye on all these men to preserve intact the uncut jewel of the family crown.

How absurd it was, therefore, that onto this scene of almost uninterrupted courtly wooing Anton Schaefer stumbled. Absurd, for courtship pertains to those who live at court, that is, to royalty, or at least to the nobility, or at the very least to the wealthier members of the lower estates. Ungainly, uncivilized Anton, his eyes popping out of his head even before he had cast them on Maria Magdalena Fromm or strained them unduly with his hemp rope, was called Anton *Schaefer*, not because his father had been named Schaefer, but because that is the German word for shepherd or for the breed of dog that tends the sheep. Anton the shepherd had no family except for the sheep he herded. No mother or father had engendered or begotten him, as far as anyone in the valley could remember, and he was visibly more beast than human being. He wore sheepskin clothing rudely sewn together with strips of sheep gut, was shod in clumsy sheepskin buskins, and carried a purse of sheep belly with a few lonely coins in it.

Had he ever spoken? Never, unless in mumbles or cries to the sheep. Yet the sheep themselves were taciturn, and Anton usually followed their lead. Even the name Anton was a local joke, since it was the name farmers liked to give to their billy goats. Billygoat Sheepherd was thus his name, or would have been his name, had he been spawned in England; as matters fell out, he was dropped by unknown progenitors in Germany, littered in the Black Forest, as though the grassy pastures were mother to him and the fragrant pines his sire.

His wanderings brought him and his flock to the mouth of the Möhlinbachtal every March. Each year, the people of the village grumbled that he had arrived too soon: the fields were still under snow, even at the bottom of the valley. Higher up, a full meter of icy slush smothered the incipient thyme, wild sorrel, and sheep's yarrow.

—All that white you see on those sheep isn't wool—it's snow! laughed Frau Kühn, pointing at the flock and its shepherd.

—He'll ruin the Bishop's herd, replied Papa Fromm gravely each March.

Yet every year, miraculously, the snow retreated as the herd advanced, one mass of whiteness giving way to another. Each year the peasants could measure the promise and the fulfillment of spring by the lumbering pace of Anton Schaefer and the steady progress of his rambling, ravenous sheep.

Anton was a good shepherd. He and his dog Struppi kept the herd and the springtime advancing step by step up the valley. Time and the seasons, all in good order, held sway—until that fatal year when the sheep arrived halfway up the valley at the pastures of the Bonnihof. Maria Magdalena Fromm, now thirteen years old, was loitering in the doorway with two of her maiden friends. Their laughter trilled like birdsong in Anton's alert, erect ears. His bulging eyes swept across the pasture to the girls. His animals grazed. He gazed. The sheep were unperturbed. He was perturbed. Anton was suddenly too warm under his sheepskins. Even the soles of his feet were suddenly too warm, too moist.

It was not that Anton felt the proddings of an animal urge. All his life he had felt animal urges alone, and he had given in to them like any sensible beast. Cold, he sought warmth; hungry, he ate; thirsty, he went to the stream. No, what happened when Anton saw Maria Magdalena for the first time was that he began to feel human. From that instant on, the journey to the end of his tether was a brief one. He knew by instinct, as it were—although of course it was not an instinct—that he dare not cross the pasture and go to her as though to a stream or a fireplace or a loaf of redolent bread. All his brief life people had taught him about the invisible fences that separated him from them. Fences of blood, fences of religion, fences of caste and station, fences of liquid capital and real estate. Anton Schaefer knew his place was at the backdoor and in the barnyard: he was human enough to know that.

A sensible sheep shakes its woolen head to scatter the flies that pester its eyes. Yet Anton stared and stared.

What no one knew, what no one could say, was whether Maria Magdalena returned the shepherd's gaze, and if so, for how long and with what import. The two girls who were giggling with her did see her attention wander for a moment; they followed her look out across the pasture, but they saw nothing there except a flock of sheep.

—Spring is on the meadow! We'll be weaving garlands of flowers soon! cried demure Ulrike.

—Stinky Anton's on the march! cried gay Waldtraud.

Maria Magdalena did not let herself be distracted for long. At least, that is what Ulrike and Waldtraud told the abbot and the local sheriff many months later. Maria Magdalena herself told them nothing. Indeed, from that Christmas morning when she went into the cow stall to toss the morning hay until the end of her brief life, she said nothing. Nothing to her father, nothing to her confessor, nothing to her younger brothers and sisters. She might have said something to her mother, had the measles not swept the woman away two years earlier.

Maria Magdalena had seen death at close range. She had tended her mother to the bitter end. Nothing about deterioration and death had been withheld from her; she was innocent of no dire detail concerning our mortal condition. There was only one way to account for her silence after that Christmas morning of discovery. Her father, Helmbrecht Fromm, had long suspected it. He remembered that at midnight on Christmas Eve, with her ear pressed against the wall separating their sooty kitchen from the cow stall, Maria Magdalena had heard the cows speaking. There was nothing unusual about that. Yet on this particular Christmas Eve—the onset of her last year on Earth—the cows had muttered incomprehensible things, impossible things, which the girl had heard not so much through the cavern of her ear as in the entrails of her tender body.

—The animals are saying that mother misses me, the girl told her father. They say that mother has become a sheep.

Madness in those days was viewed as possession by the devil. Helmbrecht Fromm did not yet know the form that this devil had taken, although for months now he had suspected. And he certainly knew madness when he heard it.

—Your mother is dead. She is in heaven. Anton has turned your head.

At that very instant, out in the tenebrous stall, amid the murmur of the lowing cows, Anton was turning his own head, turning his entire body again and again, slowly back and forth, breathlessly forth and back. Having at long last put on his full humanity, Anton now became the perfect Christian.

Had he actually told Maria Magdalena that her mother was a sheep? Is that what he had whispered through the thick whitewashed wall that separated the kitchen from the cow stall and hayloft where, months earlier, they had made the most innocent and tender love? That seems highly unlikely. For that would have made Anton and Maria Magdalena something like brother and sister, inasmuch as Billygoat Sheepherd himself had been, as far as anyone knew, spawned by the sheep. And he clearly did not want Maria Magdalena to be his sister.

Or is that not what every look of lovers across an open stretch of grass means? Two human beings of either sex or any and every sex discovering something like kinship? A kinship destining them to the embrace? One severed twin looking for another, seeking to reconnect? Ancient comedy, tragedy, and philosophy agree on asking that question.

Who can explain precisely how they came together? All we know is that Maria Magdalena taught Anton how to speak, which is what a lover always does for a beloved, and that Anton taught her about the sheep, which is what only the rarest of humans can do for the other. Maria Magdalena taught him speech by placing his fingers on her mouth and lips. He did not understand.

She finally gave him his own tongue by letting him borrow hers; she grew more and more silent as he became truly eloquent and spoke in tongues. He taught her the sheep's muzzle, showed her those unutterably tender lateral concavities immediately behind the nose before the wool starts to curl and thicken, and demonstrated how the ewe communicated to her lamb by nuzzling. He showed her where the lambs took their first nourishment on a winter's night before they were old enough for the zesty grass of spring. He showed her whence and how they had been born. He showed her all these things not by pointing to any sheep—for he had left them to graze in the pasture above the Bonnihof under the watchful eye of Struppi—but by showing her on herself how these things were ordained. She was too amazed to be frightened. And she saw that he was afraid enough for the two of them. All the chatter of the local princes and potentates, all the boastful pratings of the journeymen and wealthy farmers' sons, all the machinations of the masters and the monks were neutralized now by Anton's sheepish speech. His bulging eyes and fumbling hands became precious to her. She confused all his demonstrations and all the feelings these demonstrations aroused in her with thoughts touching her dead mother, as though every ewe were a "you" and all tenderness were one.

Hence, Maria Magdalena's words on that Christmas Eve, words that convinced her father that she had been possessed by the powers of darkness. Yet she was not possessed. Certainly not by Anton, if only because shepherds have no possessions. For his part, Anton may well have succumbed to possession. Now that he had been given a tongue, he began to speak to everything out in the fields—to trees, clouds, his sheep, his dog Struppi, and even to the grass on which the sheep were grazing.

—I know why you are so green! he would cry, careless of whether or not the grass replied.

—I know why you are so tender! I know why you are so wet in the morning!

Maria Magdalena's brooding father needed no evidence to convince him. He organized the people in the village, especially those people who had daughters, into a mob that soon pursued Anton high into the hills. Yet Anton knew of the old silver mines in those hills where the righteous would never find him, and he hid himself and held out through the long summer and fall of 1625, abandoning his lair only to spy on his beloved Maria Magdalena in the Bonnihof far below. She, for her part, at every opportunity gazed longingly up into the hills. Sometimes she looked right at him without seeing him. He was making the transition back into a wild thing, becoming once again a creature of nature. And he almost made it.

At about Christmas time, however, he came down from the hills, careless of his safety, goaded by memories of sweet spittle and speech. In the dark of night, he headed straight for the Bonnihof stall.

He waited.

She did not come. Her father had taken over the evening chores. Anton hid.

The last thing Anton Schaefer heard in his mortal life was a debate among the cows.

—But today our Savior is born!

—Not for Anton . . .

—For us all! It would be a terrible sin!

—Not for Anton. Not for Maria. Her mother is a sheep. They both must go to her and receive her blessing.

The discussion was still going on when Anton's roughshod feet slipped off the edge of the loft and launched him into the eternity of a village's vague yet undying memory, its memory of the lover suspended in the rafters. We avert our eyes now in order not to have to see him in all his wretched splendor. We leave that terrible vision for Maria Magdalena to endure on that Christmas morning, as she did endure it, until on the following Christmas Eve, at the end of 1626, precisely at midnight, and on the explicit instruction of the cows, she wordlessly followed her shepherd. That, at least, is what the villagers of Sankt Ulrich say.

On doing good

Thoreau is a baddie. He hates goodies, despises do-gooders. He scorns them as vociferously as Emerson does. The writing of both authors is never spicier than when a do-gooder turns and burns slowly on the spit. It is as if both authors had met William Faulkner's "Cora," from *As I Lay Dying*. Probably they did, at least in prototype. In Thoreau's case, the matter of doing good first shows up in "Economy," and it runs like a red thread—or a red cape— through all of *Walden*. At the outset, not long after he has lambasted his elders, Thoreau writes: "The greater part of what my neighbors call good I believe in my soul to be bad, and if I repent of any thing, it is very likely to be my good behavior. What demon possessed me that I behaved so well?" (W 7). In this regard, Thoreau is a perspicuous forerunner of Nietzsche and Freud, each of whom has his own ideas about the origins and ends of benevolence. It is doubtless time to read these bad boys again, now that we have become convinced once again of our moral excellence.

In "Economy," Thoreau confesses that he has "indulged very little in philanthropic enterprises" (W 53). He hasn't the genius for it, he says. "As for Doing-good, that is one of the professions which are full" (ibid.). For the amateur like himself, good has to be a kind of by-product, a lucky accident. "What *good* I do, in the common sense of that word, must be aside from my main path, and for the most part wholly unintended" (ibid.). Much later in *Walden*, he confirms this point: "Only what is thought said or done at a certain rare coincidence is good" (W 250). The good is like the sun, Plato says: if you confront it directly, you will go blind, so that others will have to do good to you. Philosophers and preachers have long debated what Plato means when he observes that the good is "beyond being," but the usual result is that they claim privileged access to the Beyond, wherever it may be; they have a hotline to the Good, or to the Infinite, as they often prefer to call it, and a moral police force at their beck and call to enforce its law. Philosophers who preach goodness are not kings but tyrants—petty tyrants, to be sure, tempest-in-a-teapot tyrants, but tyrants nonetheless.

There is a less pleasant reason to spurn goodness and the good, however, and Thoreau now unloads on us his olfactory account of the do-gooder:

There is no odor so bad as that which arises from goodness tainted. It is human, it is divine, carrion. If I knew for a certainty that a man was coming to my house with the conscious design of doing me good, I should run for my life, as from that dry and parching wind of the African deserts called the simoom, which fills the mouth and nose and ears and eyes with dust till you are suffocated, for fear that I should get some of this good done to me,—some of its virus mingled with my blood. (W 54)

Is this merely the haughty New Englander's inability to accept generosity, or is it the deep-seated hatred of self that causes the Puritan to drop to his knees and bleat with Wayne and Garth, "We are not worthy! We are not worthy!"? In that case, all this fuming and fussing against the do-gooder would be just another instance of the Good. An embarrassed child of the Good—a challenged child, to be sure, marked and marred by all the family traits—but a child of the Good in any case.

That it may be more than haphephobia—fear of being touched by the good—is suggested by Thoreau's example of the Jesuits who did good to the native American tribes by converting the tribes' prisoners of war who were under torture. "The Jesuits were quite balked by those Indians who, being burned at the stake, suggested new modes of torture to their tormentors" (W 54–55). The editor of the Variorum edition adds a dry, disturbing note (W 274n. 214): "There are many such incidents recorded in *The Jesuit Relations and Allied Documents*. See, for example, Vol. XVII, p. 109 (Cleveland, 1898)." When we examine *The Jesuit Relations* as instructed (17:87–111), we find that Hank the Heathen (sorry, Henry the Protestant) exaggerates. It isn't that the Jesuits relished torture for its own sake. Indeed, they scorned the heathen savage who practiced it. Yet torture proved to be the only surefire guarantor of Election and Predestination. Whereas the missionaries did reasonably well with sick babies and the doddering elderly, they batted eleven for twelve with torture victims of all ages. "I guess I'm heaven bound," quipped all but one of the dozen enemy braves beneath the branding iron or in the scalding pot. The service performed by the Jesuits reminds me of the good done by Pope Pius XII and the Vatican Secretary of State at the end of World War II, when they helped many German politicians and military personnel get a clandestine fresh start, providing them with visas and safe conduct to various countries of South America. Charity covers a multitude of war crimes. But back to Thoreau.

Thoreau is no Prometheus; philanthropy is not his thing. Selfishness? Perhaps. Yet Thoreau replies by exhibiting to us the covert selfishness at the heart of so much advertised generosity. "I believe that what so saddens the reformer is not his sympathy with his fellows in distress, but, though he be the holiest son of God, is his private ail" (W 57). Think of the contemporary preacher of "community" who dependably proves to be out for himself, consistently tooting his own horn and elbowing his way to the front of the line; think of the preacher of "duty" whose duty proves to be milking the system for all it is worth—always with the cleanest conscience in the world, of course, since self-deception is here cultivated as high art. The mask never slips, at least not when the epigones of the Good happen to be in the vicinity of a mirror.

Once again, however, Nietzsche would begin to worry about the ricochet of this analysis, the recoil back onto the critic himself or herself. Experts in the kickback received by the Good, that is, those keen-sighted experts who get a kick out of exposing the secret gluttony of the good folks, will have to feel the kick of their own genealogical weapon. Bad boys who deflate the do-gooders will otherwise turn out themselves to be the Good Old Boys. Does the mask never slip? If it does not, what do the baddies know about the do-gooders? And even if it does slip, and the baddies catch a glimpse of the moral charade, will they ever be able to wield a weapon that doesn't punish the user?

Organized religion

Thoreau's exposé of doing good expands in scope to become a critique of organized religion in general—organized religion, as opposed to disorganized religion, which is an experience of holy Chaos. "Our manners have been corrupted by communication with the saints. Our hymn-books resound with a melodious cursing of God and enduring him forever" (W 57). If Thoreau were alive today, in God's Own Country, what would he dare to say? And whatever he might say, God's Own Country would surely condemn him for it. Thoreau might point out to us that in spite of *The Simpsons* and *South Park*, the unholy alliance of Christianity and the radical Right flourishes as mightily as it ever did. "Love" is tattooed on one of Robert Mitchum's fists, "Hate" on the other; if the right one don't getcha then the left one will. For the double punch of even the most appeasing religionist is all about rancor and resentment. "There is nowhere recorded a simple and irrepressible satisfaction with the gift of life, any memorable praise of God" (ibid.). The gift of life? In today's United States of America, that phrase is a signal to blow up abortion clinics and the people in them, while the Supreme Court stands back and stands by.

However that may be, *Gift*, in German, means "poison," and sometimes Thoreau's "gift of life" shows toxic symptoms. As we have seen, this messy life of ours is often too much for him and seems a "disgrace." When he decries the life of the senses and the sensual life, if only in sensual sleep, his voice is indistinguishable from the melodious cursing of God that he censures. Does he not sense this?

Perhaps he does. For among the most despicable of the "Visitors" to the cabin at Walden Pond are those "ministers who spoke of God as if they enjoyed a monopoly on the subject, who could not bear all kinds of opinions" (W 115). One may at least hope that liberality toward opinions will enable us to hear the mixed chorus of our senses, drives, and desires. Whether or not this is so for Henry David, we may be certain that he is a proponent of *disorganized* religion, seeking his faith in birdsong, his hope in solitude, his charity in merciless self-study. And also, one must note, in the relentless study of books—especially the sacred books of the East. What should the solitary man do? "Let him humbly commune with

Zoroaster, . . . and through the liberalizing influence of all the worthies, with Jesus Christ himself, and let 'our church' go by the board" (W 81). That is from the chapter on "Reading."

My own life, if I may say so, is full of religious presentiments. A friend encouraged me recently to read Paul's first letter to the Corinthians on the subject of love. Several days later she telephoned to apologize.

—When I got home I followed my own advice and read First Corinthians again. I'm sorry, Paul is a pig.

I had no way of comforting her or altering her judgment about the Apostle, except to caution her that she might be being unfair to sow and hog. In fact, Paul's sole moment of generosity, as far as I can see, appears in Romans 8, where he opens the pearly gates to every form of life and not merely to the human animal. All creatures will eventually become "children of God," he says. Of course, in the meantime you may never touch a woman, at least not after you have been born and nursed, although you may take Fido with you when you go.

As for those "children of God," even an alert four-year-old can be a member of disorganized religion, a participant in holy Chaos. In fact, the membership rolls of the Church of Holy Chaos show a serious decline after the faithful reach the age of five. By seven and the age of reason—organized, universal atheism.

Tell Marlonbrando your dreams, honey, and everything will be all right, Part Six

—Surely you, more than anyone else, must think there is something mad about my having a cat as therapist!

—You are unhappy with the way our sessions are going?

—No, they are very productive for me. But, I mean . . . therapy . . . from a cat?!

—Perfect for transference, says Marlonbrando, rather archly.

—Transfur . . . ?

—Transference, without which no analysis can progress. Without transference there can be no talking cure, no free association, no abreaction . . .

—No cure?

—No cure in any case.

—Why perfect for transference?

—You've looked into my golden eyes. What have you seen there?

—God, or Nothing.

—Exactly. Perfect for transference: an absolutely blank screen on which you are free to project whatever your unconscious heart desires.

—There is a certain feral wisdom about you . . .

—Flattery will get you no free sessions.

—Tell me about your method. Are you a Jungian? For I see in you the archetype of an Egyptian deity. An Adlerian—a proponent of the will to power? Or are you more the cigar-chewing, straight-shooting Freudian type?

—Life is simpler for us felines. We are not as sectarian as you humans. For us, a mouse is a mouse, a method is a method.

—You make it sound as though your patients are mice.

—Cat and mouse? As good a definition of transference as any.

—And I? Am I a man or a mouse?

Marlonbrando smiles a smile I have never seen before, unless in *Alice*. He keeps his thoughts to himself.

—Forty-five minutes, he murmurs.

Living in the present

J. Glenn Gray, one of the wisest friends I ever had, once warned me that I had too much of myself in the future. There are also people who have too much of themselves in the past, he said, or in the present.

—But you have too much of yourself in the future.

—What do you mean? asked the indignant young man, his hazel eyes flashing.

—Your projects mean so much to you that when they go awry you lose all patience, he replied, his blue eyes smiling.

We had been working together on a publication project, and our ship now appeared to be foundering in rough seas somewhere between the German and American publishing houses. I was mildly hysterical, perhaps with the *m* of *mildly* inverted, and Glenn was trying to restore some sort of balance.

One wonders at—and about—the twenty-eight-year-old Thoreau, who apparently managed to live so fully in the present, consigning the past to history and leaving the future to tomorrow. Something tells me that he was a bit more concerned about his own publication projects, his own *texts*, than he admits. Does he not at one point call them his *excursions*? Even so, he prides himself on his capacity to loaf, to meet the day with indolence and to savor the present. "We should be blessed if we lived in the present always and took advantage of every accident that befell us, like the grass which confesses the influence of the slightest dew that falls on it; and did not spend our time in atoning for the neglect of past opportunities, which we call our doing our duty" (W 237).

By contrast, Heidegger says that human beings are *always* projecting themselves on their possibilities, throwing themselves into their ploys and plots and plans, so that they are inevitably propelled toward their future—at least until they reach their ultimate possibility, which is death. We are essentially pro-jectile, according to Heidegger, shot from guns like puffed wheat, hot with our latest schemes and bursting with our future. I believe him, because that is how I am and always have been, as far back as I can remember. I imagine Heidegger on vacation as Magritte imagines Hegel on holiday, warding off the rain with an umbrella but collecting the rainwater in a glass perched precariously on top of the umbrella, having it both ways with the monstrous power of the negative, collecting material for his next project. And Heidegger? He thinks of his future in terms of authenticity and resoluteness even on the beach, even on a cruise, even in a poolside hammock sipping Piña Coladas, no matter how intensely Thoreau begs him to relax: "In view of the future or possible, we should live quite laxly and undefined in front, our outlines dim and misty on that side; as our shadows reveal an insensible perspiration toward the sun" (W 245). Dim and misty—a rarefied and even vague future that waits on the action of the earth, moon, and sun—that is how Thoreau wants his life.

Can we follow him? We would have to learn a new sort of passivity, because we have always been so nuts to be agents. Granted, Thoreau too is often an agent intellect of a mole-like kind: "My instinct tells me that my head is an organ for burrowing, as some creatures use their snout and fore-paws, and with it I would mine and burrow my way through these hills" (W 73). An organ for burrowing? That is what all the philosopher–excavators say. Yet my lover disarms me by saying that my head is flesh to be kissed or an empty barrel to be clobbered. Kissed, by preference, on brow, cheek, and lips, if the lips are patient and silent enough to wait for it. A new passivity? Where do we learn that? In tremulous proximity to a first kiss, says the Romantic philosopher Novalis, since that is where philosophy begins. (Plato's *wonder* is Novalis's *kiss*.) Novalis writes: "I wish my readers could read my observation—that the beginning of philosophy is a first kiss—at the precise instant they were listening to Mozart's 'When Love Shines in Your Blue Eyes' being performed with passion, if indeed they were unable to be in tremulous proximity to a first kiss" (2:331). He adds: "The lips are so important for sociality; how very much they deserve the kiss. Every soft and gentle elevation is symbolic of the wish to be touched" (2:407). The kiss gets my present underway precisely by my having to wait for it. Forced kisses are untimely, too early, too late, precipitous, retarded.

Is that the secret of the better balance Glenn wished for me? No wonder I didn't understand it! The Overachiever was being asked to wait for something no agent could activate. Hölderlin, that beautiful man and great poet, dreamed of such hard-won patience. In a late poem eventually entitled "Mnemosyne," dedicated to the Mother of the Muses, Memory, he writes (CHV 1:437):

. . . And always
A longing sets off for the unbounded.
Yet much is to be retained. And fidelity is needed.
But forward and backward we will
Not want to look. Let ourselves be cradled, as
On the swaying skiff of sea.

Out of doors

It is still too cold to read and write outdoors, but once again I am out here at my blue writing table until my fingers turn just as blue. Something in me wants to escape the confines of the stube, even though I love those confines. What Henry loves most about his cabin are the chinks between the boards, which admit the blustery wind. He wants the outside inside. He is hardier than I. Yet I know about this hunger to be out there under the sky even in weather. "It would be well perhaps if we were to spend more of our days and nights without any obstruction between us and the celestial bodies, if the poet did not speak so much from under a roof, or the saint dwell there so long. Birds do not sing in caves, nor do doves cherish their innocence in dovecots" (W 20).

Even when I am out of doors, however, with no more doors to close behind me, I always heed the call home. Homesickness is the prevailing mood of philosophy—that's another thing Novalis said while he was waiting for that kiss. My friends laugh at me when, on hikes up the mountain, miles away from the cabin, I crane my neck to see if I can locate the precise spot the cabin occupies in the forest below, the spot flagged so proudly by Douglas the Fir. They would laugh more uproariously if they saw me treading the path above the cabin on the way to fetch my milk. The south wind is so predictable and so prevalent here that when I reach a particular point on the path I can smell the smoke wafting from my chimney. I always

recognize the smell—I know my wood fire as I know my cuticles—and I breathe in the wood smoke with the most profound contentment, aspirating my own indoors outdoors.

To love the out of doors is to love the doors that take us back into the interior of the house. That is the lesson we learn (though only by way of deprivation) from the narrator of Franz Kafka's "The Burrow," who is forever hovering at the secret entrance, huddling tremulously near the moss-covered trapdoor, both inside and outside his home at once—at least in his fantasy. We go abroad as homebodies even if we should feel like strangers when at home. The great outdoorsman is but a cabin boy. He never runs out of doors.

Bronchitis? Pneumonia?

That is the question, at least in retrospect. After writing outdoors one day—all day long—in the unseasonably warm January sun, I felt my lungs fill with fluid in the evening, as though from a tap. I was sick for about two weeks, unable to move much of the time, sleeping away the days, fitful in the nights. Too sick to bother with medicine, too weak to climb the stairs, I took to my sofa in the stube. Afterward, a friend who is in the medical industry told me that my symptoms indicated pneumonia. I remember that Thoreau died young of a pulmonary affection.

88

Day, season, and year

"The day is an epitome of the year. The night is the winter, the morning and evening are spring and fall, and the noon is the summer" (W 227). Whence the feeling here at the cabin that summer is gone in a trice: it is the meridian, the high point, to be sure, but the ascending arc that looks forward to the high point and the descending arc that gazes wistfully back to it describe the vast temporal arc of the day. "The moment of the shortest shadow," Nietzsche's Zarathustra calls the noontide. I notice, by contrast, that my own life—well past the meridian—is casting longer and longer shadows on the day, the season, and the year.

The bloody truth about trees

The setting sun this evening told me the truth about trees. There had been thick clouds overhead all day. The sun put in its first appearance at sunset. Its light shone beneath the cloud cover, until suddenly the monstrous Storm Beech was red veined against the sky—orange, red, scarlet, maroon, and purple—before fading to black. Fiery orange the sodden grass, bloody and brilliant the bush and the beech. Green leaves were never more green than when they were flooded by this garish jack-o'-lantern light. As the still leafless boughs of the Storm Beech went from orange to crimson, I realized that the tree was more alive than I had thought: the trunk and branches were now blood-rich arteries carrying life-giving plasma to what would later be leaves. I had always thought that it was mere sap that did this, sap being unrelated to what coursed through my arteries and veins; yet I was the sap, because I didn't realize that the tree was a blood relation of mine. These few moments of bloody truth salvaged a day that was otherwise lost to grayness. Salvation like this is a glory that makes you forget the other salvation they preach about—to have won another older sister so late in my own life is glory enough for any mortal.

—She smelled like trees! cries Benjy.

The head monkey at Paris

Henry's critique of fashion has always been one of my favorite parts of the book. Here is the gist of it:

> When I ask for a garment of a particular form, my tailoress tells me gravely, "They do not make them so now," not emphasizing the "They" at all, as if she quoted an authority as impersonal as the Fates, and I find it difficult to get made what I want, simply because she cannot believe that I mean what I say, that I am so rash. When I hear this sentence, I am for a moment absorbed in thought, emphasizing to myself each word separately that I may come at the meaning of it, that I may find out by what degree of consanguinity *They* are related to *me*, and what authority they may have in an affair which affects me so nearly; and, finally, I am inclined to answer her with equal mystery, and without any more emphasis of the "they,"—"It is true, they did not make them so recently, but they do now." Of what use this measuring of me if she does not measure my character, but only the breadth of my shoulders, as it were a peg to hang the coat on? We worship not the Graces, nor the Parcae, but Fashion. She spins and weaves and cuts with full authority. The head monkey at Paris puts on a traveller's cap, and all the monkeys in America do the same. (W 17)

Beware all enterprises that require new clothes, Thoreau admonishes, and I have always responded fervently to his admonition—by looking like a slob. Correction: philosopher. Yet something has happened to me, or several things. For one, I fell in love with someone who cares about clothes and has exquisite style and taste. She determined to dress me up and take me out. Had I persisted in my slovenliness, she would have dressed me down. The terrible thing is that I myself began to notice what people were wearing, and now I am ashamed. Why? Puritanism. I was raised to feel contempt for fashion, and whereas other portions of the Puritan program did not take, that one did. Puritanism and an undeniable sexism. I always felt that a man who paid attention to fashion wasn't much of one. With a woman it was different, of course: a woman could have style—indeed, was expected to have style—along with brains and heart. A woman could have and be everything; indeed, she was expected to be and have it all. She was both object and subject—the philosopher's dream, if the philosopher was a guy. That has not changed much, in spite of feminism. Yet the number of men who have an aesthetic sensibility is growing. I fear I will never be one of them. The Puritans will laugh over my grave and try to reclaim all of me. (But I'll see to it I'm laid out in FCUK and not in Land's End, just to give them a hard time.) Do clothes make the man? Let us not believe this cliché of the name designers who profit by it. Yet it seems certain that the power of fashion runs more than skin deep. The suspicions that Henry and I raise against fashion are therefore themselves suspect.

It is terrible for me nevertheless to have to live in the era of designer clothing, in which people feel proud to be wearing a logo on their shirt, granting free advertising to companies that can afford to pay for it. The designer dressed might as well be wearing sandwich boards. I realize, of course, that it is all about self-advertisement.

—Hi, I'm wearing a Ralph Lauren polo shirt, as you can plainly see by the snobby logo. That's because I make a lot of money and could play polo if I wanted to and if I could stay on the horse. If you could see my horrid Hilfiger underwear, you'd be even more impressed, if only by the near-miss Mondrian logo.

The long and short of it is that I am entirely ambivalent about this thing called fashion. I am like Brian preaching about the lilies of the field and the birds of the air, suddenly undone by someone in the crowd.

—'Ave the birds got jobs?! Leave 'em alone!

As a young man, I was shaped by Heidegger's indictment of the "They," *das Man*, the neutral "one" in the expression "one dresses this way now." In the room the women were coming and going talking of Paloma Picasso, and it seemed to me essential to express my contempt for all of "Them." We were all expressing such contempt at the time; one simply did so, that was all there was to it. "They" made me do it.

Now things with me have plunged to such a nadir that I find myself paying attention to fashion in shoes—the epitome of stupidity, inasmuch as all one needs is a pair of sturdy hiking boots with Vibram soles, boots that will not have been designed by Ralph or Oleg or Kenneth or Coco. Yet the very phrase *epitome of stupidity* and the catachresis with *nadir* stick in the throat of my designer pen: I'm growling "Vanity!" from the pulpit and secretly hoping that the head monkey at Paris will approve of my rags.

177

And if I bristle at the thought of my own secret hope that I may blossom as a flower of fashion, once again I hear a voice in the crowd.

—'E's 'avin' a go at the flowers now! Leave 'em alone! They're pretty!

91

On the gift-giving vice

The most terrible result of falling out of love, losing the love that once sustained us, is that we lose the person on whom we used to shower gifts. We gather sparkling stones at the beach, as in the old days, then mutter to ourselves, "To whom can I give these, if no longer to her?" And the world seems empty, seems to have lost its entire store of beautiful things. Toss the stones!

92

Losing the whole world

Is that the most terrible result of falling out of love—losing the one on whom we bestow gifts? It could actually be worse than that. For what about the sole gift they once gave us? Heidegger says that a human being shapes or forms the world. Derrida took this to mean that when a person dies, a whole unique world goes up in flames. Freud felt that this was unhealthy. Yes, we lose a *person* we love, but the *world* remains intact, he wrote. After all, you are the survivor, and the survivor inherits the world. After his daughter Sophie died at age twenty-six, and after his most beloved grandchild "Heinele" died as a young boy, Freud was not so sure about survival and not so sure about inheriting the world. Derrida insisted up to the time of his own death that each death is fatal to the world. "Each time unique," he said over and over again, "the end of the world."

Common sense cries out against this, but I sense what Derrida means. And I think that what he means applies to a failed love as well. We miss the *world* that the lover brought us. All those details of a particulate life! Part of that world may have been nettlesome, the part we called *baggage*, and we might delude ourselves into thinking that we are happy to be rid of it. But that the *whole* world they brought us should be gone, vanished in smoke and flames, seems a disaster.

Some of the Greek philosophers thought of the world's end as ἐκπύρωσις, "conflagration," "holocaust." Even if we ourselves light the pyre, hoping that the flames will consume every remnant and every memory of the love that has died, we soon stand aghast as the flames consume *everything*, so that nothing can be rescued. We are left with ruins, embers, ash.

—One has to move on, one must rebuild, say our friends, counseling the apparent survivor.

—Try rebuilding with ash, we reply.

Knowing when to break up

The end of the world is a matter of grave consequence. One must therefore learn when to break up. It is an art without parallel, and few have mastered it as I have. I will teach you. Consider it advice to the lovelorn.

At the forefront of your consciousness you must grasp, as though by the lapels, three convergent facts: the first is that the vast majority of human beings are obtuse of mind and vicious of character, heart, and habit; the second is that, in all probability, your lover belongs smack dab at the center of that vast majority; the third is that you too are human.

Good. Now you are ready.

94

Accentuate the negative

—Are you close enough to see my imperfections? she once asked me.

—I'm so close that my vision is blurred, I replied.

After that we parted ways.

When we fall out of love or, worse, when someone falls out of love with us, there is only one contrivance that will help. One has to call to mind all the flaws and peccadilloes of the former lover, the sorts of things that only the pettiest person in the world would ever have noticed in the first place. Thank goodness we were taking notes! At the time, our pettifogging shocked us; now we see what virtue was in it. For what else can help us when we are bereft? Sour grapes, you say? Dialectic, I reply. Hegel did not live in vain.

95

Prejudice

How can you know for certain whether your ex-lover is an unthinking person, petty minded, pig-headed, narcissistic, hopelessly prejudiced? You cannot *know* such a thing; you must *assume* so.

How to become just friends

When the flame is extinguished, he or she will say they want to become "just friends." They should have tried friendship while the flame was hot. Frigid air is for refrigerators, not friends. Just friends? No, not even if the *just* refers to *justice*, itself a chilly virtue, one that friends do not need.

Faithless fidelity

You betray a spouse. You break one promise, make another. You fall, in love. You and your spouse quarrel and divorce. Then, in the fullness of time, your lover lets you fall by the wayside. Or was it you who did the dropping? Can you remember quite precisely how it all unraveled? Are you certain about that? Or merely certain of hurt? One thing is sure: you can taste the bitterness in your mouth. You needn't *imagine* her or him with your replacement, because you *remember* the mobile god of love so well. Hölderlin says that divine infidelity is the easiest thing in the world to remember, because afterward you are left alone to tick off the hours in suffering. Sometimes a snarl twists that bitter mouth of yours. Often, however, a johnny-come-lately fidelity rises in you like an unknown, unwanted grace, and you are surprised to find yourself blessing the day that the illustrious god Eros was born—both the god and the one who withdrew from you, or the one you pushed away, she or he once upon a time incarnating that very god.

We will keep faith unto death. No one promised us that faith would be useful; no one promised us that fidelity would be at our beck and call.

Advice to the lovelorn

Too late. Always too late.

Books

"Books, the oldest and the best, stand naturally and rightfully on the shelves of every cottage" (W 77). The decision about which books to take to the cabin each year was also a weighty one: I had to bear the consequences—and the load—of my decisions. The only books of mine that stayed here (in the Permanent Collection, as it were) were a dictionary of the American language, a thesaurus, the *Oxford English Dictionary*, and the Oxford Shakespeare; they joined books belonging to the cabin that are still most useful to me, including German, Greek, French, and other dictionaries, along with the multivolume *Brockhaus* encyclopedia. For the rest, my immediate tasks determined the selection. At one point I had four different editions of Hölderlin's works and five of Sophocles' tragedies, each one necessary, none redundant. For chilling inspiration I had, and still have, Trakl's poems, for minor irritation and major delight, Goethe's two volumes of *Wilhelm Meister*. For personality maximization I now have Freud's works; for corroboration of my dignity as a former US-American academic I have Don DeLillo's *White Noise*, Philip Roth's *The Human Stain* and his four-volume *Nemesis*; for religion I have Nietzsche' works and letters.

If I knew or could remember the contents of these shelves over the years of all my sojourns in the cabin, they would spell out my biography, such as it is. "How many a man has dated a new era in his life from the reading of a book" (W 80). I remember asking my parents a long time ago for a special Christmas present—an English translation of Heidegger's *Being and Time*. That was a very appropriate—indeed, an ecstatic—Christmas. I believe that was in 1966, a year or so after my first acid bath in Nietzsche's works. But back to the cabin.

What other cabin-blessed books would I have to mention? Melville's *Moby-Dick* and *Pierre; or, the Ambiguities*—in fact, all of Melville by now; Musil's *Der Mann ohne Eigenschaften*, Gabriel Garcia-Márquez's *Cien años de soledad*, James Joyce's *Ulysses* and *Finnegans Wake*. Or, as Mr Jinglejoys also loves to call the last-named work, *Fillagain's chrissormiss wake, the meandertale*, or *meanderthalltale, that fanagan's week*, or *Quinnigan's Quake* and *Wimmedgame's fake*—on and on endlessly *Till Gilligan and Halligan*, finally avenging the Irish for Thoreau's mistreatment of them, *call again to hooligan.* (And, speaking of Joyce, how glorious is the memory of a Bloomsday party I was able to organize at the cabin not so long ago with students I taught in Freiburg in the mid-1970s!)

The only slightly more sober works of Novalis and Schelling have graced these shelves in recent years. *Prometheus Bound* looms there now, along with Virginia Woolf's *The Waves*, George Eliot's *Middlemarch*, just about all of Faulkner, and a very ragged copy of *Walden*.

I always chuckle when I hear that someone is "well read" or indeed has "read everything." In which languages? I always wonder. And from which centuries? How few in fact are the books we have a chance to read before we die! How wonderful it would be if we could borrow a few extra years of life on our library card!

Former inhabitants . . . of color . . . at Walden Pond

As Thoreau guides us through a bit of local history, namely, the history of the former inhabitants of the woods at Walden Pond, we are struck by a curious fact: they were mostly African Americans—men and women of color. While I am confident that African American scholarship has by now researched thoroughly these pages of *Walden* and meditated critically on them, I confess I have not seen that scholarship. And while I have nothing particularly insightful to say about these former inhabitants, it does seem noteworthy that Thoreau lives in an integrated neighborhood, diachronically considered, even though he lives there now alone. Something in W. E. B. Du Bois's *Dusk of Dawn* and in Toni Morrison's *Playing in the Dark* compels me to remark on these pages. Perhaps I am in search of clues concerning the lives of the Burghardt family (Du Bois's mother's family) in the valley of the Housatonic; or maybe I am curious to see how the Africanist presence plays with and in Thoreau's literary imagination. Or perhaps I am simply reminded of the fact that Du Bois and Thoreau share a hero—namely, John Brown. At all events, the most telling aspect of the Black presence at Walden Pond and in the book *Walden* is that it is past: whoever these African American loners were, and even if they founded families, their homesteads are ruins by the time Henry writes. The world of Walden Pond, as we find it in Thoreau's *Walden*, is a truncated microcosm of Diaspora. All that remains of these folk is folklore, a local oral tradition that captivates Henry—he takes the time to register these former inhabitants, now vanished, by name.

The first among these past presences is Cato Ingraham, "slave of Duncan Ingraham, Esquire, gentleman of Concord" (W 194). One may be certain that the esquire's descendants are flourishing in Concord even as Thoreau writes. Yet what of Cato's descendants? Cato's master built him a house in Walden Woods—presumably, though Thoreau does not mention this—after giving the slave his own family name, Ingraham. (How and when was this done? With manumission? Surely earlier—by the universally accepted custom among slaveholders? Or by the more direct intervention that Du Bois calls "the red stain of bastardy"?) No doubt the master also bestowed on his man the distinguished Roman appellation Cato, after the aristocratic author of *De agricultura*. "Some say that he was a Guinea Negro. There are a few who remember his little patch among the walnuts, which he let grow up till he should be old and need them; but a younger and whiter speculator got them at last. He too, however, occupies an equally narrow house at present" (W 195). Our editor intervenes to explain that the "equally narrow house" of the "whiter speculator" has the dimensions 6' x 6' x 3'; Thoreau recognizes the equality of the races in their mortality, which recognition is neither cruel nor ironic on his part but, you should forgive the locution, existential-ontological. "Cato's half-obliterated cellar hole still remains," concludes Thoreau, and it is graced by feathery sumac and luxuriant golden rod.

Next comes Zilpha, a name I have not found in the Roman *Who's Who?* but which does turn up in Genesis. Zilpha was the slave of Leah, Laban's daughter and the first wife of Jacob. After Leah exhausted herself giving Jacob sons, she presented him with Zilpha as a surrogate wife or concubine—who promptly granted Jacob two more sons. One may be certain that the bible-reading master gave the name Zilpha to the woman Thoreau now tells us about, although whether or not she bore children we are not told. Thoreau does not speculate on either the name or the possible "red stain," but tells the following story:

> Here, by the very corner of my field, still nearer to town, Zilpha, a colored woman, had her little house, where she spun linen for the townsfolk, making the Walden Woods ring with her shrill singing, for she had a loud and notable voice. At length, in the war of 1812, her dwelling was set on fire by English soldiers, prisoners on parole, when she was away, and her cat and dog and hens were all burned up together. She led a hard life, and somewhat inhumane. One old frequenter of these woods remembers, that as he passed her house one noon he heard her muttering to herself over her gurgling pot,—"Ye are all bones, bones!" I have seen bricks amid the oak copse there. (W 195)

Thoreau offers no enlightenment concerning the motivation of those British incendiaries, nor about the very possibility of such a deed. Prisoners of war—on parole? Yes indeed, parole seems to have been the custom back in the day, although parole with license to burn and pillage does seem odd. And there is no further commentary on Zilpha's "somewhat inhumane" existence, impressed on her by her "hard life."

The gift proffered by these former inhabitants is the occasion for storytelling and the vignette. Thoreau is a master of both. Yet his mastery is not that of the Master. It rests rather, I believe, on the deep sympathy he feels toward these neighbors. That sympathy liberates his talent for narrative and portraiture, for something more contingent, more intimate, and more *en miniature* than his grand and principled resistance to slavery, which is well-attested. Thoreau *likes* these neighbors of color, certainly more than he likes the Irish, and he likes them because they are not boring but colorful. They are characters because they have character.

We get closer to the inevitable ambiguities of color in the United States, however, as we approach Brister's Hill:

> Down the road, on the right hand, on Brister's Hill, lived Brister Freeman, "a handy Negro," slave of Squire Cummings once,—there where grow still the apple-trees which Brister planted and tended; large old trees now, but their fruit still wild and cider-ish to my taste. Not long since I read his epitaph in the old Lincoln burying-ground, a little on one side, near the unmarked graves of some British grenadiers who fell in the retreat from Concord,—where he is styled "Sippio Brister,"—Scipio Africanus he had some title to be called,—"a man of color," as if he were discolored. It also told me, with staring emphasis, when he died; which was but an indirect way of informing me that he ever lived. With him dwelt Fenda, his hospitable wife, who told fortunes, yet pleasantly,—large, round, and black, blacker than any of the children of night, such a dusky orb never rose on Concord before or since. (Ibid.)

I imagine Morrison scrutinizing this passage, suddenly looking up, then back down to the text, paying scrupulous attention to Thoreau's choice of words and wondering: Freeman? Scipio Africanus? Color/discolor? It would seem that Melville's colorless all-color White ought to be the essence of discoloration, except during the time of "white reign," when White is the constant and therefore unheard background noise, the color that no one ever notices. And what are we to say of the "hospitable wife," "large, round, and black, blacker than any children of night," the duskiest of dawns? Telling fortunes—"yet pleasantly"? One can doubtless look too hard for hidden meanings and covert prejudices and wind up projecting all sorts of things onto Thoreau's text. Yet Thoreau's interest in Fenda, and even in the romance of her darkness, does not seem to me suspect. Perhaps that is because I am a White man. But perhaps also because one has to learn to be less ashamed of attention paid to differences in race, color, ethnicity, and sex. Equality was never promoted by pretended indifference to differences. And yet one is left bemused by these vignettes of color, bemused and troubled, precisely because the former inhabitants vanish with scarcely a trace. Buried "a little on one side," close to the graves of the enemy.

Later in the chapter, Thoreau muses on those depressions in the earth that mark former foundations. His musings interest me because on the mountaintop above my own cabin, deep in the pine woods, I myself have found decrepit walls and ruined foundations. Among the mossy stones one finds the occasional implement of rusted iron. Other than that, the silence of dead centuries rests on the place—the inaudible whispers of the silent people, the farmers and workers who leave no written record to speak for them. No monuments, no gravestones, but only a rectangular boundary stone with letters carved on opposed sides, G.S.U. and HO, meaning the community (*Gemeinde*) of Sankt Ulrich and the town of Horben, a village several kilometers down the hill, where I catch my bus. Elsewhere, on another continent, Thoreau writes concerning the Concord ruins: "These cellar dents, like deserted fox burrows, old holes, are all that is left where once were the stir and bustle of human life, and 'fate, free-will, foreknowledge absolute,' in some form and dialect or other were by turns discussed. But all I can learn of their conclusions amounts to just this, that 'Cato and Brister pulled wool;' which is about as edifying as the history of more famous schools of philosophy" (W 199). Among the philosophers, Michel de Montaigne was famous for remarking that the most edifying aspect of our shared humanity is that we are *commourans*, "those who die in common," whether we pull wool for articles of clothing or, as writers, pull it over the eyes of the unsuspecting. At all events, lilac bushes burgeon in the gardens of these dispersed human households that Thoreau examines, and he thinks of the youthful hands that must have planted the slips of the bushes there, hands that had all their toilsome future ahead of them—even if "Freeman" was the foisted surname and "free-will" a double-edged attribute:

> Little did the dusky children think that the puny slip with its two eyes only, which they stuck in the ground in the shadow of the house and daily watered, would root itself so, and outlive them, and house itself in the rear that shaded it, and grown man's garden and orchard, and tell their story faintly to the lone wanderer a half century after they had grown up and died,—

blossoming as fair, and smelling as sweet, as in that first spring.
I mark its still tender, civil, cheerful, lilac colors. (W 199–200)

Diaspora and dispersion in their larger, more comprehensive forms—
the evanescence of ephemeral humans of any and every shade—draw
Thoreau's eye and focus his mind. If he sometimes shows impatience with
the Abolitionists, and he does, it is only because he knows that our shared
mortality—fate foreclosing both free will and foreknowledge—can never
be abolished. Attention to this adamantine fact, he believes, may be what
has to underlie every platform of social justice. Yet what would he think,
do you suppose, if he could watch, more than a century and a half down
the road, the video of a policeman murdering a Black man in cold blood,
and only half the nation raising serious objection to it? And what would
he think of the need to shout aloud the simple phrase—which does have
a Thoreauvian ring to it—Black lives matter?

Crooked genius, crooked rules

The independence for which Henry is so avid has but one aim: the man wants to follow the bent of his own genius, "which is a very crooked one" (W 40–41). A crooked bent is not merely a pleonasm, however; it is the way things in the world actually work. Novalis, around 1800, invoked what he called "crooked rules," *krumme Regeln*. Ever since Pythagoras, the "straight" has been esteemed and the "crooked" spurned. Yet nothing human follows a straight line, certainly not in the more complex geometries of our time. All science and all ethics have to learn to stop playing it straight. The unconscious is most assuredly zigzag, while consciousness itself meanders among the observed landmarks of multiple worlds and manifold selves. Of course, it is not enough to mutter contemptuously that everything straight lies, as the dwarfish spirit of gravity does in *Thus Spoke Zarathustra* when he insists that time itself is crooked. The bent of our genius must instead follow the minute twists and turns of every crooked path, suffering all the loops and reversals to which the regime of crooked rules commits us.

Art is not yet weaned

A new acquaintance of mine here on the mountaintop, a retired industrial designer whose father built a cabin nearby, showed me photographs of his sculptures—for he has become a sculptor since retiring a decade ago. He is a genial and ingenious man, and now he turns out to be a talented artist. I suppose I expected a series of Futurist sculptures from him: highly technical and "technicized," edgy and cold figures fabricated by this industrial designer. Instead, I saw in the photographs of his work and then later in his studio breasts and bellies cast or sculpted in bronze or carved out of cherry wood or mahogany, swollen nipples of walnut women. No machines, no hydraulic pumps, no tooling tools. All his technique (and he has a lot of it) has gone into protuberances that have been around since the reign of Chaos—that era prior to the ages of gods, titans, and human beings, when (as Plato tells us in *Statesman*, although he does not speak of Chaos as such) the human body evolved. How, now? Is art not yet weaned? Evidently not. Should we be surprised?

Art has a good memory and a sense of direction, however much it may meander. Chaos theory is only now beginning to pursue all the things that were determined during the reign of Chaos, when the divine human body, with all its protuberances and perturbations, got its start. Art has long submitted to the requirements of that reign, and it will continue to submit, as the rest of the world, gone technical, prods and pokes.

103

Life is not yet weaned

Four kids, bucks, or billy goats, were born at my neighbor's farm early this spring. He wishes there had been some jilly goats among them, but nature is not to be deterred. The last to arrive is now a little more than six weeks old. He is several weeks younger and quite a few pounds lighter than his cousins, yet they are gentle with him, at least to the extent that gentleness and goat can be said in the same sentence. Two nights ago, my neighbor found the mother of this littlest kid dead in the stall. No one can figure out why she died. The kid was sucking away at a teat of the dead mother when they found her. The kid didn't start to bleat until they took her away. Neither art nor life is ever fully weaned.

Problematic praxis

Early on in his book, Thoreau says the usual thing about philosophy, to wit, that theory must be borne out in practice. "To be a philosopher is not merely to have subtle thoughts, nor even to found a school, but so to love wisdom as to live according to its dictates, a life of simplicity, independence, magnanimity, and trust" (W 10). On magnanimity and trust, one must consult the final chapters of Melville's *The Confidence Man*, set in a paddle wheeler's barber shop, on one wall of which appears the sign No Trust. But to continue with Thoreau's unremarkable remark. To be a philosopher "is to solve some of the problems of life, not only theoretically, but practically" (ibid.). However, much later in his text, during a discussion of sobriety as opposed to "ebriosity," Thoreau interrupts the preachments of "Higher Laws" with the following confession:

> But to tell the truth, I find myself at present somewhat less particular in these respects. I carry less religion to the table, ask no blessing; not because I am wiser than I was, but, I am obliged to confess, because, however much it is to be regretted, with years I have grown more coarse and indifferent. Perhaps these questions are entertained only in youth, as most believe of poetry. My practice is "nowhere," my opinion is here. (W 165)

"My practice is 'nowhere.'" "Nowhere" is of course utopia, in this case *ou-topos* rather than *eu-topos*, no place at all, Erehwon as Ne'erwhen. Who knows but that this coarseness and indifference with regard to praxis, in spite of Thoreau's demur, may be the fruit of age—vaunted wisdom itself? At least Henry is able to see his book as a catalogue of opinions rather than of categorical imperatives or universal maxims, a fact that ostensibly places his book in close proximity to sophistry rather than philosophy. Though what could be more sophistical than the pretensions of categorical preaching and prescriptive palaver? And what could be more philosophical than the effort to discern one's limits—even the limits of sensibility, engagement, and commitment that one confronts in one's own coarseness and indifference? Higher laws succumb to lower realities, where crooked rules alone apply.

The Copernican Revolution?

Kant tells us that the very essence of modernity is expressed in the fact that we no longer look to nature for guidance in the way we pose age-old questions; rather, we humans now compel nature by means of the experimental method and all our technologies to respond to questions of our own devising. It is a strange Copernicus at work here, however, inasmuch as everything in nature is now made to orbit around *us*, as though *we* were the very center of the solar system—which is precisely the Ptolemaic view that was supposedly overturned by Copernicus, Galileo, and Kant. At all events, and these events are astronomically complicated, Thoreau resists the reduction of nature to grist for the technological mill. Most would concur that this makes him a Romantic. A few of us wonder instead whether this makes him rational. Here is how "The Pond in Winter" begins:

> After a still winter night I awoke with the impression that some question had been put to me, which I had been endeavoring in vain to answer in my sleep, as what—how—when—where? But there was dawning Nature, in whom all creatures live, looking in at my broad windows with serene and satisfied face, and no question on *her* lips. I awoke to an answered question, to Nature and daylight. The snow lying deep on the earth dotted with young pines, and the very slope of the hill on which my house is placed, seemed to say, Forward! Nature puts no question and answers none which we mortals ask. She has long ago taken her resolution. (W 214)

This is not to say that there is no science in *Walden*. Thoreau spends a lot of time on his knees, not praying to Dame Nature, but measuring the diameter of bubbles in the ice. There is geometry aplenty here, oodles of "law and harmony," and lots of mad calculus, too: "If we knew all the laws of Nature, we should need only one fact, or the description of one actual phenomenon, to infer all the particular results at that point" (W 219). Icy intellect too is at work here, rather than any faculty of affect or passion alone. In the end, the only thing that rescues Thoreau from Copernicus and

Ptolemy alike is his roving *imagination*, the Romantic faculty par excellence. For Kant too, imagination is the power of our innermost heart and mind, the power that enables us to weave the threads of rules and concepts, even crooked ones, with the dangling threads of sensation into the weft of experience. Thoreau often refuses to weave, however, and the shuttle of his loom is left to idle. That is when Henry David is at his revolutionary best, allowing his imagination to quit the loom and freely roam over the loam of the Earth.

New beech leaves

Each year I photograph them. Earlier on I used slide film, now I photograph digitally, my camera zooming in on a solitary leaf against the rising sun in May. With a magnifying or macro lens, you can see colonies of neophyte cells. Each bud opens and yields leaf after leaf, fold after fold, almost as many folds as in a woman's sex. I now lean back against the trunk of the Storm Beech and look up into the myriad new beech leaves. They tremble in the wind; they shiver with life.

God bless the American *Igel*; or, true patriotism

Last fall an *Igel* (pronounced *eagle*), which is German for hedgehog, built its nest of leaves under the stairs at the entrance of the cabin, intending to hibernate there for the winter. Throughout the winter, I feared that my crunchy comings and goings, tramping up and down the ice-laden stairs, would rouse it from its winter slumber and drive it off in search of peace. Every evening I would peep under the stairs and examine that unkempt heap of leaves, hoping that my *Igel* was still there. (Marlonbrando has just leapt up onto the windowsill, demanding his supper; he has perhaps deprived me of my little chickadees, and I just hope he doesn't touch the American *Igel*. I'll tell him: "These colors don't run! These stripes don't fade! These stars don't fall—and they sure as tootin' do the shootin'!") I had no way of knowing for sure if the hedgehog was still my nearest neighbor or if the pile of leaves was precisely that and no more.

Tonight, after an evening promenade through the fog and rain (it is May 3, but it feels like March), returning down my path toward the cabin, I saw the hedgehog waddling toward me. When *it* saw *me*, it froze. I said a few things in my ecofriendliest nonhierarchical Franciscan tone of voice, then hurried into the cabin and grabbed a carrot out of the fridge, hoping that a red, white, and blue *Igel* would accept an orange root for fodder. From the sink I grabbed a knife. Back out on the path I cut the carrot into bite-size chunks, informing my angel that this pumpkin-colored tubercle of the earth would be good for him or her. I then tiptoed back to the cabin door, not looking back, remembering Orpheus's mistake.

The patriots are right: the American *Igel* is an angel in which we should all take the greatest pride. He or she harms no one, shuns firearms, and is as cute as a button. So goes the nation, correct?

One more angel story, the last one, I promise

Many winters ago, I was here in the cabin with my twelve-year-old son. As the spring rains came on, bringing endless drizzle with endless fog, we felt the onset of a serious case of cabin fever. We donned our polyester "wet suits," so called because in them you perspire so much that even if the rain doesn't penetrate you arrive home soaked to the bone. Anyway, we trudged across the muddy pasture of the Eckhof and entered the pine woods. We were keeping quiet in case we should come across any deer, as we had a week or so earlier. We arrived at the spot in the woods that for years had supported the largest fox den in the neighborhood. In fact, we called it Hotel Zorro. We stood quietly on the path above the largest opening of the hotel, looking at nothing in particular, unless it was the curtain of grass—now pearled by beads of rainwater—that hung suspended over the opening. Suddenly, a tiny head poked through the curtain. A baby fox was on its way out, munching nonchalantly on the grassy curtain—a fox pup not more than a couple of weeks old. He or she waddled out of the den into the foggy daylight. My son and I stood like statues. The fox nibbled at the grass, gradually nosing his way toward us. He, if it was a he, had the short snout and round head of every infant. His coat was a fluffy rust brown, his eyes a bright blue. He ambled right up to us, stopping about four or five centimeters from my right boot. He sniffed the boot curiously, then looked up into our eyes. We could see the shock of recognition on his face.

—Oh, shit. This is what mother has been warning us about!

He turned tail and scrambled back the way he had come and vanished through the beaded curtain into the dark of the den. As he hurried off, we noted his tiny triangular ears and mere stump of a tail. We could have scooped him up and taken him home with us. But you don't scoop up angels.

All the way home, and for the rest of the day, my son and I were in a daze, due to the epiphany, unable to believe that we had really encountered the littlest angel. Our neighbors, when we told them the story, were jealous, in the way that the Israelites must have been jealous of the prophets after they came down from the mountain with stories of visions.

Creationism

God made each species special, his special creation granting each species specific talents. To human beings he specifically gave intelligence, philosophy, and science, along with the capacity to be especially unaffected by all three.

Capital punishment

To select nations God gave the special right to carry out capital punishment on their citizens. They are, as I remember, Iraq, Iran, North Korea, Saudi Arabia, China . . . and there's one I can't recall.

May fog

In winter and early spring, the fog formed ice wings. Now, in late spring, it sews diamonds onto the tips of every needle of pine and fir. It has been raining for over seventy-two hours without interruption, a vertical rain intersecting the horizontal drizzle of the fog. The fog is so thick you can cut it with an air hammer—then, suddenly, when I look up from my misty page, the fog is gone. The most succulent green, suffused with the electric yellow of new life, now replaces the philosophic gray on gray of the fog. The perfect new leaves of the maple, as big as fans, drip with rain.

—Don't worry, they seem to say. This rain could go on for weeks. Our parents told us about it before they dropped, all spotty and torn, last fall.

The sandy, stony earth, covered now with plush grass, fern, and wildflower, is somehow able to absorb all the rainfall. There is no erosion that one can see, although puddles and rivulets form everywhere. On the shores of each puddle, blackbirds help the nightcrawlers onto their feet.

All this I can see from my window. I look out over my newly designed and installed Zen Rock Garden toward the greening Storm Beech. A magnificent view—until, glancing up from my page a few moments later, I see that the fog has returned, thick as putty. My Zen garden is now Hawai'i viewed from five thousand feet in a gale. On the steel roof of the cabin, the never-ending beat of the rain, like the snare drum of *Bolero*, though with wilder syncopation.

Thoreau's model farm

He's having an open farmhouse. Let us see who will make an offer on Thoreau's model farm:

> Farmers are respectable and interesting to me in proportion as they are poor,—poor farmers. A model farm! where the house stands like a fungus in a muck-heap, chambers for men, horses, oxen, and swine, cleansed and uncleansed, all contiguous to one another! Stocked with men! A great grease-spot, redolent of manures and buttermilk! Under a high state of cultivation, being manured with hearts and brains of men! As if you were to raise your potatoes in the churchyard! Such is a model farm. (W 149)

At long last, here is some muck that Henry will bless! Indeed, he blesses it with Whitmanian exultation—or is it with Emersonian irony? It is hard to tell. In Amish or Mennonite country in Pennsylvania, Ohio, Indiana, Illinois, and Wisconsin (I bicycled through Wisconsin some years ago), you will see farms as spick-and-span as the Black Forest farms that surround me here. They too are redolent of manure and buttermilk, although the incomparable sweetness of straw underlies and ameliorates it all, like the base of a heady perfume. The only spoiler for the nose here in the valley is silage, to which more and more of the larger farms are turning. Silage spoils the scent of the aged urine that has been sprayed generously across the fields. It makes the cows' milk taste like cheese before cheese is made from the milk, whereas the milk that flows from a cow fed on honeyed hay, the hay that sprouts through the brown crust of *ur-alt* urine, is the purest liquor.

The hay harvest will come in June, which may seem early, but you have to remember that the grass has been growing since mid-March (hopefully not since January: *Wächst das Gras im Januar, wächst es schlecht das ganze Jahr*—"If in January the grass grows tall, the rest of the year it won't grow at all"), and by late May, it is reaching for the sky. Those first warm nights after all that rain work wonders. A second hay harvest will come in August, the so-called *Öhmd*. The grass will be finer then, and fuller, more feathery, richer and sweeter, though harder to catch in your rake—it blows away in tufts through the tines. A single day of work at the hay harvest or on the *Öhmd* is worth a year of academic study and teaching. Not because of some Tolstoyan fantasy about the peasants but because in one day you collect enough fodder to feed your neighbor's cows for many weeks of winter. And the cows are so grateful.

The farmers here *are* poor, at least in comparison with other classes of people in this affluent Germany of the twenty-first century. Yet they are rich in so many ways, even when one desists from romanticizing. When Rüdiger tells me about his day at work in the city—it is evening now, and he is out here feeding his goats—it is plain to him and to me that the goats are more rewarding company than the city dwellers. True, the goats bless you with the occasional bump, but unlike people, they don't impale you with rudeness.

Stocked with *men*, Thoreau says more than once. What about the women? The women of a Schwarzwald *Hof* work incredibly hard. Not one of them has hands that will serve for a photo spot. Yet more than their hands suffer. Before the forester's wife was sixty, she had to have both hips replaced. The wheelbarrow full of barn sweepings that she struggled with every morning and every night took its toll on her. I remember seeing her grappling with the wheelbarrow one day, whereupon I volunteered to assist, but . . . I don't want to talk about it. In spite of the toil—or because of it, who can say?—she has a cheerful smile and a friendly word for everyone.

There is no model *modern* farm here, none that produces mad cow disease with the most up-to-date technology and artificial cannibal feed. (Elsewhere in Germany and throughout Europe and the United States, the skeletons of slaughtered cows are ground up and fed to the cows who are the living heirs of the slaughtered—that is how the disease spreads; by contrast, when cows eat grass instead of grandparents, they do not go mad; that is ancient wisdom—you can find it in Pythagoras and Empedocles.) Everything is old-fashioned here—obsolete, I suppose—seat-of-the-pants and salt-of-the-earth. You can get milk, raw milk, so rich that overnight it separates out, with the top third of the bottle full of thick cream. I don't tell the farmers this, but I sometimes cut the milk, adding almost equal amounts of fresh cold water. That way my cholesterol merely soars rather than skyrockets. Apart from worries about cholesterol, you can drink the milk with joy rather than fear. And you can get your eggs from chickens that are not tortured inmates, your unfiltered honey from dedicated local swarms, your bread baked in a wood-burning oven, your butter and cheeses of various sorts from several farms hereabouts, and your trout from the pond at the forest's edge. No model farms, it is true, but here one can eat and one can live.

113

The water works

My drink water flows down from Schauinsland Mountain. I use it, after it is pumped from the village well across the meadow up to the cabin, for my tea and coffee, for my shower, for my laundry. And for drinking. No chemicals go into the well—except for a bit of calcium, since the water, according to a testing lab, is "too soft." But no chlorine, no hydrogen peroxide, no whatever. Friends and family who visit the cabin invariably remark on the water, its freshness and good taste, its "sweetness." Along with the air up here, the water is the greatest blessing on my life. The air invigorates, and the water works.

There is nothing inorganic

Thoreau inherits this extraordinary doctrine from Goethe and Schelling, perhaps by way of Coleridge. For centuries prior to and following the great Romantics, we have on the contrary accepted the proposition that everything is dead. The lifeless machine rules, from the muffler shop to your doctor's examination room. My doctor once smiled his most ingratiating smile at me before he spoke.

—You have to realize that I most often regard you as a sack of chemicals.

—I didn't know you cared, I replied.

How it changes things to think of water and metals and gases as alive! A preposterous animism or hylozoism—as long as one refuses to think about it. "There is nothing inorganic," affirms Thoreau (W 233). "The earth is not a mere fragment of dead history, stratum upon stratum like the leaves of a book, to be studied by geologists and antiquaries chiefly, but living poetry like the leaves of a tree, which precede flowers and fruit,—not a fossil earth, but a living earth; compared with whose great central life all animal and vegetable life is merely parasitic" (ibid.). The new ecology is surely teaching us that the radical interdependence of part and whole, which has long been the customary way of defining the living, characterizes every corner of the universe, whether telescopically or microscopically considered. True, the mechanicians are in the labs decoding the last gene, or so they promise us and so they firmly believe, having already reduced it all to the dead; yet we can be confident that when the last tabulations are in on the first decoded gene, that gene will have mutated, and the mechanicians will have to start mowing the lawn all over again. Life will prevail—even if human life does not.

There are disadvantages to a civilization that treats everything as though it were already dead. We give death such a head start, no wonder killing wins the race. Imagine instead a science and a culture that assumed *the living* as the basis of knowledge! Learning, as the application of crooked rules, would be metamorphosis, that is, a readiness for change tempered by a sense of care and carefulness within the nexus of life—where life is both parasite and host. We might even become more reluctant to kill one another.

That would be both miraculous and paradoxical, inasmuch as death has traditionally been defined as reduction to the inorganic. In other words, the hypothesis that there is nothing inorganic does not mean that death is ruled out and that everything is permitted. Albert Camus will have been closer to the mark when he says that that *nothing* is permitted, in the sense that no deed has absolute sanction. Everything has a claim on our care. As we live and die, so does all else, though at first we fail to recognize the blood relation and the family resemblance. There is nothing inorganic.

115

The ashes of once living things

Nietzsche must have been listening to Goethe and Schelling, if not to our Henry. In one of his notebooks, he writes the following: "Our whole world is the *ashes* of countless *living* creatures: and even if the animate seems so miniscule in comparison with the whole, it is nonetheless the case that *everything* has already been transposed into life once upon a time, and so it goes continuously. If we suppose an eternal duration, consequently an eternal alteration of all forms of matter—" (KSW 9:472–73). The unfinished thought appears to be that *lifedeath*, written as one word, is endless alteration and alternation, yet in each of its moments eternal reconfirmation.

The katzenjammer of birds

By five in the morning, they will have started—blackbirds first, because they hardly ever stop. Earlier, it was only the occasional goat bell, whether soprano or alto, accompanying the tenor and bass cowbells, that startled the night. The ruckus of birds will soon wake you, you know it, and so your mind starts to anticipate. You hear them twittering in the ticking of the clock downstairs, as though in the hills of northern Japan. They fly in a westerly direction across the Sea of Japan from Sapporo to Vladivostok, sailing on to northern China and the Mongolian steppe, across Lake Balkhash of Kazakhstan, over the Volga and the Don, casting shadows over the Black Sea, which is named after them, through the Ukraine into Europe. They rattle the mountains of Moldavia now, and now the Rumanians can hear them, and the Serbs, Czechs, and Poles. Their hullabaloo sweeps across the "former East" of Germany, past the Danube and the Bavarian Forest to Lake Constance. Now they are on your very threshold. You scramble out of bed before their earsplitting song and the foot stomping sun can rouse you.

The wolf spider

Lycophobes and arachnophobes unite! Unite and beware! You have nothing to lose but your nerve—and face! The cabin is full of spiders, winter and summer, spiders seeking warmth, spiders seeking cool shade, spiders seeking whatever the cabin has to offer. None of them is as terrifying as the wolf spider, however. An educated person, it is true, learns to love every aspect of nature, no matter how terrifying or sublime. Yet I affirm what a former student of mine cried when a June bug landed on his shoulder.

—My love of nature ends where bugs begin!

I am better educated than he, clearly, since with me it is only ticks and spiders that induce immediate hysteria. Oh, and scorpions, of which there are thankfully none in the Black Forest. But especially the wolf spider, of which there are regrettably plenty. It hides in the funnel-shaped web it has spun in some convenient crevice of nature or culture. You can see—if you are crazy enough to get close—its two front legs poised for the leap. Touch the web with a stick too vigorously and those jagged legs retreat; touch it lightly, as a fly would, and you are in for a surprise. The wolf spider is *quick*. Arachnophiles say it is quick because it must seize prey efficiently. I say it is quick because it wants to scare human beings to death.

Last week I came home from a journey to the north of Germany. I had closed and bolted the shutters before I left, and now I went to all the rooms of the cabin to open them. In the bedroom, I opened the east window and unbolted the shutters, pushing them halfway open to admit a shaft of light. A gigantic wolf spider darted across the ledge, scrambling this way and that, looking for a place to hide. Had it turned right, it would have plopped down onto my featherbed and spoiled a year's worth of sleep. It stopped; it calculated. Ever so slowly, I pushed the shutters all the way open. The beast plopped over the other side of the sill into the great outdoors. Presumably, it dropped two stories to the ground, but I didn't worry about its safe landing. I checked the underside of the outside sill to see if it had cunningly scrambled beneath it instead of leaping to its death. Of course, I saw nothing. After a final check, I closed the windows tight and went to the medicine cabinet for a nerve tonic—the essence of essence, my central heating, my sweet Serotonin Schnapps.

A morning hike

I damaged my knee while skiing last winter and have been recovering slowly ever since. On this morning in late May, however, I was up at five, and as the dawn showed a clear sky I determined to test the joint. I hiked to the Kohlerhof, then up the ridge of the Obermünstertal to the Giesshübel, then back home—about six or seven hours in all, a long walk or a modest

hike for a weak-kneed would-be author. I took my little red notebook with me and went nuts with notes. I soon realized that I was trying to record a whole world of things seen, heard, touched, smelled, tasted, thought, remembered, imagined, sung, or spoken and that even if I had infinite time and infinite skill I could not jot it all down. For on my walk there were infinities within infinities, as Leibniz says of every drop of water in a pool: in every droplet, in each fragment of stone, and underneath each scale of every fish lie concealed another pool, another stone, another scale of another fish, another entire universe. In short, I would be recording a few selected highlights in the flood of my perceptions and thoughts, whereas it was the steady stream of lowlights on my hike that I most wanted to capture, step by step, across gravel paths and grassy meadows. At any rate, here is a transcription of my notes.

Weeks ago the flashy dandelions promised the more subtle yellow of buttercups—more subtle, though each cup glistens with butterfat—and now the buttercups are here. Along with the dandelions, which seem to last forever, they alter the meadow fundamentally. For it is no longer green, as it has been since March, but all the hues of gold.

I come across a whole field of wild geraniums. From a distance, it looks like a field of lavender in Napa or in Provence. The early morning sun, on the oblique, illumines the petals from beneath: a purple so purple only the wine grape is more red. A purple so red, only the first violet crocus of spring is more blue, inasmuch as the profusions of spring fuse all the colors.

There is Queen Anne's Lace, one of my mother's favorites, I believe because of the name. (She also loved Lily of the Valley, which she wore as a scent.) And there is *Bergkraut*, "mountain weed," which must be a kind of wild carrot, judging from the taste. Its compact white blossom imitates Queen Anne but is not so regal; its feathery, light foliage is bitter—the cows will not eat it, wild carrot or no. At the corner of Cold Water Wood, I leave the sunny meadow and enter the cavernous forest. How much cooler it is in here! And damp! Water drips from every surface. My nose begins to imitate nature.

At the top of the rise beyond Cold Water, where the path goes left and right at a T-junction, a deer bellows its throaty bark like a dog with emphysema. Too much smoking in the den. I turn to the right, heading toward the Kohlerhof, and walk past an almost vertical stream of water—not quite a waterfall but a cascade down a steep wall of mossy stones, some large, some small, the stream tumbling, splattering, dribbling its variegated water music. The music never stops in summer; in winter, the ice merely mutes it to a gurgle.

I pass the moss-covered boulders near Priory Rock. They are no longer covered merely with lichens and mosses, as in earlier years, but have graduated to more advanced forms of vegetation. The moss has supplied enough soil for what I call "false huckleberry," a hedge that looks just like blueberry bushes (no, not Bloomberry) but bears no berries. And, rising out of the hedge of false huckleberry, true white pine and spindly gray mountain ash. The pines could well grow to enormous size after I am dead, since the march of vegetation—from lichen to moss fern hedge seedling sapling and monster tree—is, if left to prosper, progressive and unstoppable.

The gravel road, wide enough for a logging truck, is lined with *Waldmeister*, "wood master," our woodruff (*Asperula odorata*). Its tiny octopetaled white flowers shine like stars in the night sky, its delicate fingers of leaves extend in open wonder. Hereabouts, folks gather this medicinal herb for a "May Bowl," which is either an acquired taste or an excellent way to spoil a bottle of white wine, depending on the progress you have made in your acculturation.

At a curve in the road, where the brook spreads out to overflow its banks, I can smell Grizzly Leek, and so I go in search of it. ("Grizzly Leek" is my translation of *Bärlauch*, though it may not be the official English name for *Allium ursinum*.) It is a form of wild garlic, unmistakable not so much by its delicate white hexapetal blossom or by its long shiny spear of leaf but by its garlicky bouquet. If you collect the leaf in late March or early April, before the plant goes to flower, you can make a wonderful pesto that will last you through the summer and fall on into winter and the following spring. The leaf looks like Lily of the Valley, albeit glossier, and a poor old woman here died last week after enjoying a bowl of Lily of the Valley soup. (Don't tell my mother, but the Lily is deadly. Recall Mae West in *My Little Chickadee* singing "Willy of the Valley": "And believe me, boys, I can dally in the valley," coos Mae.)

In a dark grove of beeches above the Kohlerhof, a cuckoo sings its deep-throated, velvety song, as mellow as Saint-Saëns. I have twenty-five Euros in my pocket, for lunch and beer, and local folk wisdom tells me that I will be rich. Of course I will be rich! I already am a prince among men if I have twenty-five Euros to spend on my lunch and a beer or two.

A "vineyard snail" (*Weinberg Schnecke*, or, across the Rhine, escargot) retracts its tentacle eyes at the sound of my boots. I know how it feels: I have been in crowds. I consider whether or not I should move it off the road, not because of the logging trucks, which are rare, or because of the hikers, who are careful, but because of the killer mountain bikers, a species of predator unfortunately on the increase here in the Schwarzwald, but I let the snail do its slimy thing. These are the snails that go so well with butter and garlic and parsley in France; here they go best with Grizzly Leek Pesto. I recall that even though in Germany they are called "vineyard snails," in Spain they are harvested principally from graveyards, not vineyards. Never mind. Heraclitus says that Dionysos and Hades are the same.

Now that the *Bärlauch* is past, I am more attentive to all the smells. The moldering must of dead leaves in November, the bitter cold odor of Nothing-at-All in January, but now the heady smell of verdure, the sweet garland of greens in May.

A solitary deer, a large doe, leaps out of the bushes to my right, takes the breadth of the gravel road in one bound, and disappears among the spindly beeches to my left. Even though in a couple of seconds I am at the spot where she crossed, she is long gone. I look at the beech saplings, then at the elephant legs of the mature beeches farther on, and I remember what the Germans call the spindly ones—*sons o' beeches*, of course. I consider briefly whether here in Germany the death penalty will be introduced for punsters.

A monstrous hare hops up the treeless hill to my left. The Germans do not generally clear-cut, as the Americans do, but this whole hill was denuded of its gargantuan beeches some five years ago. The hare is light brown in color, with dabs of dark chocolate on the tips of its ears and on its tail. He lopes lazily, one eye on me, apparently unperturbed, unhurried.

I've been noticing the stone path markers for some time now. On the ridge that divides the Obermünstertal (to the east) from the Möhlinbachtal (to the west), these are boundary or property markers: rectangular granite stones with the coats of arms of the bishop of Staufen (to the southwest) and of the communities of Kirchhofen and Ehrenstetten (to the northeast). On the bishop's side of the stone, I can make out the familiar episcopal crosier. I can also read the dates on the worn surface, the oldest stones dating from the 1720s and 1730s. Farther up the ridge is one that is clearly marked 1723. I wonder how the old bishop is faring these days? The forest no longer belongs to him, but he has no doubt invested in the Bank of the Holy Spirit and is flourishing.

The Münstertal is a vast valley, far more generously appointed than the Möhlinbachtal: the valleys of the Black Forest become grander as one heads eastward toward the high plateau that stretches from Döggingen to Villingen-Schwenningen. The train ride from Freiburg to Donaueschingen (where the Danube starts) has to be one of the world's most beautiful train journeys, even though it takes only a couple of hours.

I am standing on a rounded hill that is covered with the smoothest, softest grass, just above the Kohlerhof, on my way to lunch. My gaze drifts

from the shocking pink pinwheel flowers at my feet—even the name of these flowers is bright: *Geranium lucidum*—to the top of the inspiring Münster Valley. I am heading toward the inn at Stohren called the *Giesshübel*, which means something like "the water pump," or "tap," or "well." I pat the twenty-five Euros in my pocket and remember the promise of the cuckoo. Prince for a day, I will tap the watering hole well.

Music of the rain

It is such a cliché that it embarrasses me to write it. Yet it is elementally true, and the sign of this truth is that when the rain falls I shut off the music of my Home Entertainment Center. Not even Gould playing Bach, not even Bernstein conducting Mahler, not even Dawn Upshaw singing any damn thing she'd like, she is so wonderful, can compete. It has been raining now (it is early June) for two days and three nights without interruption, feeding the grasses and flowers to the bursting point, many of them hip high by this time. We hayed only half of the Barley Stalk hillside—the forester knew that the rain was coming and he didn't want the hay rotting in sodden stacks. He calls this "the moist period of June," no doubt an understatement, but one that explains all the weddings. The fog is so thick that I cannot see beyond Douglas the Fir. His branches reach out their furry fingertips into the silvery blur—he himself is a sylvan blur. I have to light a fire these days, a small one, mornings and evenings, to fight the damp. I revel in the environmentally incorrect pleasure of opening the east window of the cabin after lighting the evening fire, to attend the chamber concert of the rain—a suite with occasional tympanic blasts and flashy polyphonic illuminations in the vaporous sky.

Tell Marlonbrando your dreams, honey, and everything will be all right, Part Seven

—You've been having some fun with me, haven't you?

I pretend I don't know what he's talking about. He has somehow learned—has he been sneaking a look into my private notebooks?!—that I have been toying with the idea of dropping him as a therapist and making him instead the director of the FBI, that is, of the Feral Bureau of Investigation. Marlonbrando gives me a knowing smile, the knowing grin of the Old Boys' backroom. He raises an eyebrow and continues.

—Feral Bureau of Investigation?

—All in fun. Don't take it to heart . . .

—You are betraying something of your negative transference there.

—You said you were a blank screen and I could make of you anything I wanted.

—You've been projecting little montages of yourself all over me.

—Naw, it was just stuff I made up.

Marlonbrando gives me that omniscient, infinitely taciturn smile. He always has the upper paw, with claws drawn.

—Tell me something, he says quietly.

—Anything! I reply, trying to make a joke of my dependency.

—Thoreau seems by now to have disappeared from your book.

Marlonbrando catches me unawares. I don't know what to say. He continues.

—I can't remember the last time his name came up.

Neither can I, but I do not say so. Marlonbrando scarcely pauses; he is on a roll. I feel him slapping me from paw to paw as I scramble to escape.

—You were always more sympathetic to Melville, anyway. Thoreau was just an excuse to get to Melville.

—So?

—So, why didn't you have the courage to go directly to Melville?

—I'm not in his crowd.

—Not in his class, you mean. But Thoreau? You can have some fun with him, dishing out the rough treatment he bestows on others. Sweet revenge—until you realize that this makes you just like him. Always needing someone to knock down a peg or two so you can clamber one rung higher.

—I admire Thoreau. He's a cranky bastard, but he can write.

—That he can. That he can.

A discomfiting silence ensues. I break it.

—Do you really think I resemble him?

—Observe the nature descriptions. Look at the horrific puns. Note the desire to be trenchant. The desire to compete, defeat, and crow.

—But at least I'm not so prudish.

Marlonbrando has been waiting a long time for me to say that, a very long time, and now he goes to his reward like a cat to the brimming saucer.

—All those dreams you've related to me. . . . Not a single erotic dream among them.

—I have them. I just don't tell you.

—Indeed. You want me to think you're a good little boy. You think I can be fooled? You think I haven't lived the life of a beast? You think you can fool the FBI?

—Forty-five minutes! I cry.

Save your hay

I open the door to the oblique rays of the early morning sun and all I can smell is hay. After a few days of pause due to the June rains, everyone in the valley is mowing hay again. It is like the feeding frenzy of sharks, but its result is an air pungent with the fruits of the earth—esculent grasses. We don't often think of grass as the rudimentary form of our bread, but elementary bread is what it is—at least if we are talking about real bread and not the spongy foam rubber from Wonderland. Grass is aboriginal grain. When I help with the hay harvest, I always reach a point of accelerated appetite when I want to drop down on all four and commence the repast. I want to start munching, holding back none of my ancestral bovinity. After all, it is the tiny spark of bovinity within us that makes us humans different from all the other animals.

It is all in the nose, a hay fever become brain fever, this feast of cut grass steaming in the sun. Anyone who has ever mowed a lawn, which is suburbia's vestigial organ of the hay field, knows of this allure and of the temptation to get down to it and become real again. When the temple prostipriestess of old Uruk has to humanize Enkidu so that he may become a brother to King Gilgamesh, she teaches him the arts of fermentation: bread is grass plus ferment, wine is fruit juice plus ferment, and sex is tender amiability plus ferment. Without the levity and levitation of these ferments, without the wisdom guarded by the professional virgins, we would be plodding creatures, heavy of heart, dull of mind.

All of that is up my nose this heady morning as I say "Happy Birthday!" to my son Davidcito, who is six thousand miles away. Four days from now the boy, now a man, will join me. I also anticipate the approaching fixed-date festival of Bloomsday, June 16, celebrating, among other things, Bloom's paternal concern for Stephen—symbolized perhaps by the Bloomberry bush my own father gave me in my dream. They say that the higher-order functions of the brain, such as metaphor, were in the early days—Enkidu's days—devoted to the sense of smell. Cut hay is the gnosis of noses. There is a wisdom in hay, and one must both savor and save it. You might marry an immortal horse someday. Or, if not, someone of your own kine.

A day's journey

My son and I had been hiking in the remote Maderan Valley of central Switzerland, climbing up to, and onto, the Hüfi Glacier. His flight home to Chicago was to leave Zürich the next day at mid-morning, and so we started our hike back down the valley toward the car (which we'd had to leave in the village of Bristen many kilometers below) at four o'clock in the morning. We walked by flashlight under the Milky Way and more stars than we had ever seen. As the flashlight was fading, dawn came up in the Alps, as in a tone poem by Richard Strauss. We plunged into the woods, crossed streams and fields, hurried to our car, drove carefully down the narrow switchback road to the autobahn at Amsteg and on to the Zürich airport. He flew with the sun, of course, so that he arrived in Chicago just two hours after leaving Zürich. He spent a normal afternoon and evening in Chicago and slept in his own bed that night. Perhaps he dreamt of Maderan Valley stars, or of fitful flashlights, or of the amazing lives we lead nowadays.

Dream and catastrophe; or,
the politics of archaeology

Do not dream and catastrophe often stand in close proximity? Proximity to the point of intertwining? I am thinking of the intimate relation between our hopes and what smashes them, ever since Eve and Adam bit into the apple—the instant after a serpentine Yahweh bit into the two of them. Always and always our Paradise has been bound up with stories of our ejection from it. Paradise is always and from the outset Lost. The Golden Age is ever the dream of gold, silver, bronze, and iron men and women dreamt by men and women of baser matter—in our own time, of plastic. We are the Styrofoam folk, the throwaways, the effluvia, the forlorn, fantasizing a past we hope will return as our future. Visions of the future are always complicit with a covert return to a past, a past from which we appear to have been cut off by some catastrophe of nature or culture. Because we cannot return to such a past, which never was truly present, and because we can never really recapture it for our future, our visions of that future go up in smoke.

. Catastrophe is the inclination of human temporality. Whatever goes up must come down, whatever converges must descend. This is the fate of all politics but also of all archaeology. For both politics and archaeology enliven their present and future with dreams of the past. When the archaeologist dusts off the shards at Pompeii or on Santorini or Samothrace, he or she is gazing into the mirror of archaeology's own dream and desire. That is why these imagined sites of utopia—of the lost Atlantis—hold such fascination for us, and why we are so invested in them. After the catastrophe of their loss, they serve as the magic mushrooms that inspire the ecstasy of our dreams.

124

And then the sky fell

It had been dry and hot for weeks, more Sahara than Schwarzwald. Even the most phlegmatic farmer had his hay in by this time. It was a brilliant August afternoon. Five o'clock came and went. Distant thunder was the first sign of what was afoot, so far off it seemed a kettledrum roll you aren't really meant to notice, as in the opening measure of Sibelius's Seventh. And then the sky fell.

I was sitting at my table in the stube, eating my supper, looking out at the Storm Beech. Into the blue sky, pouring down from above, I watched an alchemical mixture of black and gray clouds—pouring, literally pouring like thick cream from a pitcher, swirls of gray and charcoal cloud, until the

interval between earth and sky was as black as night. It suddenly seemed to be ten at night, which is when it gets dark here this time of year.

Then the rain started. Then the hail started. Hail pounded the roof, and the roof growled in reply. Suddenly the fields—a few moments before nothing but brown stubble—were white with snow. Not snow, really, but golfball-sized hail, the kind of hail you hear about in stories but almost never see. Rivers formed out on the grassy path that leads down to the cabin. The cabin's rainspouts and gutters threw in the towel. A dripping noise in the bathroom told me to get all the pots and pans out of the kitchen and into the bathroom fast. I placed the pots as though on step patterns at a dance studio, but the drops from the ceiling were clumsy dancers, all over the place. And the dark! With all the lights out and all the plugs pulled from their sockets! And then the fragrance, which made it worth all the fret and fright, the smell of wet earth, parched earth now quenched, drenched, saturated! And the coolness of the air! And the gradual brightening of the sky, the second dawning of day! Too many exclamation points!

The sky was still up there, as it turned out, but it wore a sheepish look, like Chicken Little. And then, inevitably, spoiling it all with biblical and ancient Greek mythological kitsch, a rainbow brighter than any that was ever seen before on earth, and the sun shining through!

125

Still more work

We remember that Thoreau went into the woods to work out that "private business" of mourning: the death of a brother about whom he remains so silent. Did no one else in his vicinity die while he was in Walden Woods? Was he called to no funerals, no burials? Was there only that very safe literary history ensconced in the ruins of farmhouse cellars or "dents" thereabouts? A secure literary history behind him and the stable horizon of transcendental eternity ahead? Is it that double confidence which makes him from time to time so brusque?

On a Thursday evening in August, more than a dozen years ago now, two young men from the village were killed in a head-on collision on the road near Hansmartinhof. Two sons of two different innkeepers, as it turned out, one a mature man on a motorcycle speeding uphill, the other the youngest son from the inn nearest the church, who was ripping downhill on a mountain bike without a light. It was August, and the dark was coming down earlier every night, announcing the darker time ahead for these two.

I did not know the older man well, but the boy was close in age to my own eldest child. The boy was a stutterer all his life, a stutterer and a stammerer, the worst in my experience. I met him on the Birkenwäldliweg one day last summer. He was on his bike, and he stopped for a chat. I asked him three questions. I wanted to talk to him, and I wanted him to know that I wanted to talk to him and that I would take the time to listen. He answered briefly. The exchange took thirty minutes.

The boy played the guitar well, and he taught himself to play the church organ. Probably he shifted the gears of his bike dexterously, without a hitch. He had a sweetness of demeanor that belied his intelligence, his wit, and his disability. The older man, the motorcyclist, was killed almost instantly—whatever the physics of their vehicles might suggest to us—whereas the boy survived for several hours in the hospital, eventually dying of internal bleeding. Scarlet flowers now mark the spots, a brief bouquet on either side of the road.

Life stammers on

He was Billy Budd, that boy. It didn't occur to me until the postman spoke to me at the funeral, and I noticed that *he* was stuttering. He had never stuttered before the young man's death, it seemed to me. He never spoke much at all, true, but he never stuttered, either. Now he stutters. Is he harboring the dead boy's ghost? Is that how life goes on, and on?

Pinions

As I walked through the woods early this morning, returning from Frau K.'s with my still-warm breakfast milk in hand, I heard a sudden clamor of wings overhead. I did not spot the bird at first, for it was already moving fast. Yet I could hear the deep whistle of its wings—this was no silent owl—as it threaded the tips of the tree branches toward the open air. The whirr was so thrilling, even terrifying, that I knew it was a huge mouse buzzard, in English the "common" buzzard (*Buteo buteo*), which an American will sometimes call a chicken hawk. (And once, I did see a mouse buzzard plummeting out of the sky onto one of Frau S.M.'s chickens, which it would have carried off, too, if her dog had not intervened.) The buzzard commonly has a three-foot wingspan, and you always entertain the most serious thoughts when you see one on its perch, especially if it is waiting for roadkill. Hearing that monstrous sound over my head, hoping he was plowing the air rather than plummeting toward me, I thought of the poetic word *pinion*, which Keats and Shelley used, but we cannot. Yet sometimes we need old words, old bottles for older wonders.

The logic of error; or, a modest disquisition on the synthesis of being, time, and truth

As I stepped out of the forest into the morning sunlight, I descried in front of my neighbor's cabin a solitary cow.

—It must have broken through the pasture fence, I thought to myself.

Cows don't do that as often as goats do, but every now and then their bulk takes them through the wire and its electric tickle, which must feel to them like just another fly. The truant animal was not yet fully grown. It was a yearling, I could see that, because its udder had not yet dropped. The position of the front hooves was relaxed yet firmly planted.

—I hope it doesn't start when I come up behind it, I thought to myself.

I had to come up behind it in order to reach the path to my own cabin, where I intended to call the trout pond man and tell him to let the Eckhof *bueh* (*Bauer*, or farmer) know that one of his yearlings was on the loose and might be lonely for company.

When did the first shadow of a doubt arise? I don't know. Yet after only a few more steps I realized that what I was looking at were two neatly trimmed beech hedges, one simulating the rump of the animal, the other its small-horned head. The trunks of the trees were legs, curving at ground level to form hooves. Fence posts contributed two more legs to the arboreal animal.

Did I belatedly "doubt" and then "realize" in my "mind" what I was "truly" looking at, or did I simply look more attentively? That is the tricky old question, older even than Descartes—indeed, as old as Plato—deployed by professors to get kids interested in philosophy. Nowadays, it is used to trick them into a cognitive science or psychology major. The only thought-provoking treatment I have seen of this question as to how we correct our mistaken perceptions, how we discover our falsehoods *as* falsehoods, appears in an old lecture course given by Martin Heidegger. The course is not so much concerned with falsehood as it is with what falsehood tells us about the truth of our situation. Heidegger conjures up the following example, which is close to my own experience of the bovine bushes.

I am walking in the woods, says Heidegger. Suddenly, I am awakened from my reverie—perhaps about a professor who one day accidentally drops a piece of chalk that falls into the breast pocket of his blue serge suit and who spends the rest of the hour looking for it on the floor while continuing to lecture on Hegel's logic—by the appearance of a deer about thirty meters ahead.

—There's a deer! I exclaim to myself.

I fix my gaze on the spot and move stealthily toward it, leatherstocking style. When I get within about ten meters of my "deer," who is remarkably tolerant of me, she turns out to be the play of light and shadow on a moss-covered boulder. I was deceived, animating the stone with visions of phantom game.

My being deceived presupposes three things, says Heidegger. First, in taking the boulder for a deer, I have in fact encountered *something*. A tendency to discover things in the world is always already at work in me, even when I am daydreaming about professors on my walk through the woods; the world, for its part, gives itself (though with reservations and never completely) to my explorations and musings. Second, such giving or rendering exhibits a temporal horizon and a temporalizing tendency. The situation that is circumscribed by my being in the forest has always already created a horizon of expectations; these expectations display the warp and woof of past and future experiences in the fabric of my present. What I *might* confront in the forest is already significantly delimited. When I see something move in the woods ahead of me, I am not likely to mutter a mathematical explanation or exclamation.

—Here comes the cube root of sixty-nine!

Unless, of course, I am an exceptionally gifted Pythagorean mathematician. Or unless I am caught up in an Expressionist painting by the Swiss artist Erhard Jacoby, which portrays in (sur)realistic fashion a "deer crossing" on a modern European highway. The highway stretches into the infinitely remote vanishing point of the picture. The familiar international sign for "deer crossing" appears on the right, as it should. You and I are in the painting too—at least, our shadows jut into the lower half of the painting, shadows cast by the sun behind us, which is apparently quite low in the sky. Emerging from the forest in front of us, just beyond the sign, in stately procession across the highway, are a family of wild boar, an elephant, a rhinoceros, and a brontosaurus.

Third, and finally, the things that *are* present in that part of the forest where I happen to be—the pines, birds, rocks, mosses, ferns, and bushes—themselves form the horizon of my expectations. In other words, even when I am being deceived, I am having to do with things themselves and not with phantasms of the mind. The point of all this is a serious one: falsehood, once it discloses itself *as* falsehood, reveals the coherence of experience—the tendency to discover things in context, the temporal structure of this context, and the presence of beings themselves, which are neither "concepts" nor "representations." Falsehood, far better than truth, exhibits to us the synthesis of disclosure, time, and being.

Okay. Okay. I'll end the disquisition. And, in truth, I'm only glad that when I stepped out of the forest into the morning sunlight I did not espy the asymptotes to the hyperbola on the loose. Their infinite approximation would also have revealed the mysterious weft of being, time, and truth, but it would have come close to spoiling my day.

Tell Marlonbrando your dreams, honey, and everything will be all right, Part Eight and Last

—And so where, in all this, is *Walden*? Are you in Massachusetts or the Black Forest? Or are you the skinny squirrely guy in the red tassel cap and geeky glasses who has wandered a bit too far? What is *Walden* to you? A child's entertainment? Where's Walden?

—I'm not sure where it is, or even what it is. It is something between walking and writing. It is something about a few very simple things—a desired intimacy with life, I suppose. I haven't been able to write about it very well here. Not consistently, anyway.

—An intimacy with solitude rather than life.

—Perhaps. But even the visitors I receive here are solitaries. It is important to keep everyone else away.

—Listen to the great democrat!

—What can I do? Ours is the Age of Encroachment.

—And you are looking for a place to hide? A place to avoid disappointment? A place to pluck raisins?

—A place without television in any case, except for the view far down the valley. A place without telescopes, except for scoping the stars. A place without telephones, except for hearing voices from afar—children, neighbors, friends, a lover.

—You are trying for utopia?

—It's like those signs advertising "Last gas station for 150 miles." This is the last refuge for my finitude.

—Well, then. You are the American Adam after all, dreaming the American Dream on foreign shores?

—If you like. Look for a red tassel cap in the east window. Look for a guy with geeky glasses. With a gray cat on the sill.

Cabin smells

They don't all emanate from me. They don't all arise from either the culinary or ignominious works I effect here. Some are exuded by the floor and walls of the rooms themselves, each room wafting with its own fragrance. These odors are remnants of the house ghosts—of all who have inhabited this place since its construction, from the shopkeeping couple to the medical doctor who escaped to this place to read, write, and think—along with the world of nature. Does the room get the morning sun or the late afternoon sun? Are the pines closer or farther away? The importance of what I do within the walls pales by comparison, except for the pine fires that I build, no doubt following a long tradition.

There is a front entrance smell, however, that represents the whole house, all its rooms, as though by synecdoche. Whenever I return to the cabin after a long absence and unlock the door, that smell puts me in mind of my son, who was here with me during my first long stay, more than two decades ago now. The cabin retains smells of him at twelve or thirteen— smells or memories of smells, who can smell the difference? Sometimes the ghosts of the past have more future and more fragrance than we do, and they will bury us, at least if all goes well.

Desperately sad

I don't know what piece of classical music I was listening to when my son posed a question.

—Doesn't that sort of music seem sad to you, *desperately* sad?

It did not, and I said so. I could not imagine what he meant or how he was hearing it, although I have to concede that I often pause before I put on some classical piece because I'm not sure I am up to its rigors. Or is my son right? Is there not always a *basso continuo* of sadness beneath even the jolliest tune? Georg Tintner says that Anton Bruckner's Eighth and Ninth exhibit strains of *tragedy* that the earlier symphonies do not, and he means that as a word of praise. He is thinking too perhaps of Gustav Mahler's endless variations on tragedy throughout his symphonies and song cycles. Alexis Zorba takes his zither down from the wall whenever he is sad or pensive, and when the beautiful widow is killed he dances. We laugh when Janis Joplin begs the Lord to buy her a Mercedes Benz, her friends all have Porsches, she must make a-menz, yet behind the raunchy tune and the biting satire lies the wretchedness of our material daze, and Janis has to sing it in order not to cry. It is as though every song is a song of the earth, every tone having an undertone of parting and farewell, desperately sad. As I mentioned earlier, both Schelling and Nietzsche wrote that classical tragedy was born from the spirit of music. That may still be so, even when the Home Entertainment Center is playing *Ob-La-Di, Ob-La-Da.*

Self-confidence

It takes so much courage for a grown child to confide in a parent, to confess some primal fear—of the blue depths of the sea, for example—when what even a mature child craves is resplendent public courage, courage enough to impress the impossible-to-please parent. When such confessions come, the parent feels alternate flashes of helplessness and pride. In a word, love.

133

Polonius

"I have a daughter," he tells Hamlet. Well, I have two, in fact, a singer and an actor. Elena Sophia visits the cabin mostly in winter, at Christmas time; Salomé Maria visits in full summer. One transforms the walls, the other the trees. One completes the hearth, the other the sun. One is a beacon in the dark, the other a firefly over the meadow. Together they constitute the seasons, round out the arts and the hours, and, together with their brother Citos, they complete the circulation of the blood. Proud fathers are a contemptible thing. Yet that is a piddling price to pay.

134

Sea of fog

It looks like November even if it is late August. Up here at the cabin, the morning sun commands a brilliant blue sky. Down below, where the hills reach about five hundred meters above sea level (as the expression goes), a sea of white fog stretches out to the invisible horizon. The sea of fog has in fact made a shoreline of the hills. The hills are now the atolls of an archipelago, with bays cut deep into each island, the pines growing right up to the water's edge. There are ebb tides and flood tides, of course, and as I write, the sea is rising. Rising at a rapid rate. Last night the moon was full. All felt the lunar tug. The sea of fog still feels it today. The sea is rising and the women are menstruating. Wait. Wait. I drown.

Sunworshiper fog

Sometimes that sea of fog sweeps upward from Günterstal and heads toward Schauinsland Mountain—only to fold back on itself in smoky swirls as it climbs. It rises higher and higher, like a bear begging for peanuts, rises until it attenuates in the sun, its wisps and pallid streaks eventually vanishing into nothing at all. You couldn't drown in it if you tried.

Weather can be extraordinarily precise

It is evening, and I am sitting bathed in sunlight outside the rear cabin wall. In front of the cabin, not more than thirty feet away, it is raining steadily. I am entirely dry. Oops. Oops. Ink blotches on my page. Not *always* precise!

137

The man in the moon

When I was a child, I could never see him, could never make out the features of his face, no matter how precise the adults' indications were. Now I see him several times each lunar month, at least if the night sky is clear. I see him at the full, popping over Schauinsland Mountain like the world's largest lottery ball. And now I notice that his expression varies from appearance to appearance. Tonight the August moon is troubled: the man in the moon is smiling as always and looking askance as always, but this time there is pain and chagrin about the eyes, including that gaping middle eye, the eye of Polyphemus.

What can have happened? Perhaps he caught a glimpse of things here on Earth as he came over the horizon? Or perhaps there is some disquieting interior confusion about whether he is a she? In German, the moon is masculine, *der Mond*, in the Romance languages she is feminine. Why is no one decoding his or her chagrin? The poet Hölderlin says that the moon rises "in mourning and in splendor." But why mourning? And why are there no professional "readers" of his or her splendid and marvelously animated face? We have so many psychics and palm readers—surely someone ought to have specialized in lunar psychology by now! Or am I the first? Ah, at last! A vocation, a calling! Psycholunalysis!

Breaking News
Marlonbrando confesses all!

Noted Thespian and feline Marlonbrando shocked the world (in the environs of Sankt Ulrich) today with his confession.

—I'm not a psychoanalyst, never have been. As for the FBI, I am not now nor have I ever been a member.

—What are you, then, if you are none of these things? demanded the sole remaining reporter.

—I was raised in a barn, just as all my teachers used to complain. I am a barn cat—nothing more edifying than that.

—But your thick gray fur and your marvelous vocabulary! exclaimed the reporter in disbelief.

—I grow this coat every winter. It's automatic. Same with the vocabulary. I shed them both come spring.

Marlonbrando waved off all the remaining questions of an importunate press with a peremptory paw. He leapt from the windowsill and loped up one of the two divergent roads toward the yellow wood, the Storm Beech aglow in the evening sun. He slowed to a stop, looked back, and offered a final explanation. It was in fact the only explanation he had ever offered of his comings and goings.

—I'll have mice-to-go before I sleep, he murmured.

And then he was gone.

Extra-vagance

Henry David has *vagance* to spare. He loves to wander, not only down to Walden Pond and beyond, but also in his writing. He shares with Emerson that glorious insouciance concerning the connection (or lack of connection) among his sentences. Each declaration is on its own, so to speak, not merely poised for the rhetorical leap but already sailing headlong through the air. It is as though the writer has to pause after each sentence until the astonished or baffled gasps among his readership die down. This is truer of Emerson than it is of Thoreau, but Henry David is happy to emulate his Concord neighbor.

Yet what am I grumbling about? It is the declamatory style of both authors that has always drawn me to their essays. Besides, if a single sentence doesn't capture an insight, what makes me think that stringing together a series of tone-deaf assertions into a monotonous paragraph or monograph will? The fact that so far I have, in the main, written academic books means that I have always placed my faith in stringing. If only I could learn how to string select words into a pearl of a sentence! But back to our talented vagrant, who can and does do some fancy beadwork.

Extra-vagance is a word for the very best things in Thoreau's book. Alongside the usual trappings of his Transcendentalist "Conclusion" ("Direct your eye inward," "Explore thyself," all the dreary hand-me-downs of our Puritan ancestors), we find gems of extravaganza. Allow me to string some of Thoreau's pearls.

"The universe is wider than our views of it" (W 242). Thoreau's cosmos, though psychologically without profile and often affectively flat, is rich in natural detail. It makes up in ponds and fronds what it lacks in dreams.

"Patriotism is a maggot in their heads" (W 243). It is not enough to know that patriotism is the last refuge of a scoundrel, which is truer than ever, and which reveals how many millions of scoundrels there are in God's Own Country; nowadays we need to know that the flies of the marketplace (I mean the honeybees of the "free market economy") reproduce as the larvae of chauvinism and xenophobia. To say nothing of our thickest and most destructive worm.

"How worn and dusty, then, must be the highways of the world, how deep the ruts of tradition and conformity!" (W 244). It was Nietzsche's and Heidegger's (and Darwin's, Marx's, and Freud's) merciless tracking of those ruts—the production and distribution of false problems and inane claims that go on leading an independent existence for centuries—that seemed to me so exciting when I was young. Such tracking, the fine art of genealogical critique, still seems crucial to me now. One may be off hamburger, but that is no reason to leave the sacred cow in peace. Or, to alter the offensive metaphor, it is better to travel to India in order to relearn worship than to slaughter in the names of the known gods. Ruts and conformity and maggots in the head—or the wider universe that challenges all our views of it: there is your Thoreauvian choice. Extra-vagance, going the extra mile, even when it comes to homecoming.

"I left the woods for as good a reason as I went there. Perhaps it seemed to me that I had several more lives to live, and could not spare any more time for that one. It is remarkable how easily and insensibly we fall into a particular route, and make a beaten track for ourselves" (ibid.). Of course, we still find the customary braggadocio: conduct your life as Henry wants you to and "new, universal, and more liberal laws" will enact themselves all around you (ibid.). And you won't be lonely, either. Old chanticleer perches on the apple-tree table at the end of his book and crows for the edification of his neighbors. In between the ruts and routes of the Thoreauvian familiar, however, hide the semiprecious stones. Such as the following jewel (W 245), which, the Resistance tells me, is going to be draped as a banner across Capitol Hill in Washington, DC:

AS IF THERE WERE SAFETY IN STUPIDITY ALONE.

Or perhaps this should become the first line of a new national anthem, or a verse added to Woody Guthrie's "This Land Is Your Land." (True, it would have to be sung as Dylan would sing it, with a few syllables left to dangle outside the melody.) Yet the Thoreauvian context of this remark on stupidity is not the American Dream transmogrifying into the World Nightmare, at least not exclusively. The more encompassing context of Thoreau's remark is the art of *interpretation* and making sense of a *text*—as we understand these things in the English-speaking world. Not everything in the passage is easy to understand, and that is quite fitting.

> It is a ridiculous demand which England and America make,
> that you shall speak so that they can understand you. Neither

men nor toad-stools grow so. As if that were important, and there were not enough to understand you without them. As if Nature could support but one order of understandings, could not sustain birds as well as quadrupeds, flying as well as creeping things. . . . As if there were safety in stupidity alone. I fear chiefly lest my expression may not be *extra-vagant* enough, may not wander far enough beyond the narrow limits of my daily experience, so as to be adequate to the truth of which I have been convinced. *Extra vagance!* it depends on how you are yarded. The migrating buffalo, which seeks new pastures in another latitude, is not extravagant like the cow which kicks over the pail, leaps the cow-yard fence, and runs after her calf, in milking time. (Ibid.)

You were looking for the sacred cow? There she flies! And, as it turns out, she—and not the cat—plays the fiddle as well: "I desire to speak somewhere *without* bounds; like a man in a waking moment, to men in their waking moments; for I am convinced that I cannot exaggerate enough even to lay the foundation of a true expression. Who that has heard a strain of music feared then lest he should speak extravagantly any more forever?" (ibid.).

This last assertion, on music, goes by too fast. It has to be read several times, da capo, as a rondo: "Who that has heard a strain of music feared then lest he should speak extravagantly any more forever?" Music may not be desperately sad, at least not always, but it is certainly always extravagant. Thoreau invites us to recall that in the aesthetics of Kant and Hegel, those demigods of the tone deaf and the lame foot, music occupies the lowest note on the scale of beauty: philosophers are instructed to clamber ever upward, chucking all the music, dance, imagery, and poetry out of their language, until they lose themselves in the dizzying stratosphere of the *concept.* I remember years ago watching a bumblebee climbing a blade of grass on an Alpine meadow. Things went well the first half of the way, but then the bee's own weight caused the blade to bend forward and him to tumble onto his head, whereupon he would circle about and start to clamber up that identical blade of grass all over again. He kept this up all afternoon, and I presume he is still falling on his head even if no one is there to watch. Much of philosophy is like that.

Thoreau's style at its best is a musical extravaganza, a grumbling basso continuo with endlessly inventive melismata trilling above. And even when Thoreau the writer is not at his best, there is nothing common about his

text—certainly nothing commonsensical. "Why level downward to our dullest perception always, and praise that as common sense?" (W 246). Because it is democratic? Yes indeed, if democracy is based on the principle a teacher of mine once expressed as "One idiot, one vote." Common sense dictates a single meaning, a simple meaning, for even the most complicated things. "In this part of the world," observes Thoreau, "it is considered a ground for complaint if a man's writings admit of more than one interpretation" (ibid.). Henry at least desires to be as large as Walt, so that he too might contain multitudes. And if he chastises his readers for being merely half alive, only those who are half dead at the top will insist that he is wrong. "There is not one of my readers who has yet lived a whole human life," he says (W 251), as though quoting Aristotle and Sophocles, the ancient authors who forbade us to proclaim a human being happy until he or she is dead. (Aristotle suspected that even the dead continue to be vulnerable—because of the reversals their children may suffer. An absurd notion, that, but I love it above all others.) Furthermore, says Thoreau, what is true of individuals may also be true for our species as a whole: "These may be but the spring months in the life of the race. . . . We are acquainted with a mere pellicle of the globe on which we live. Most have not delved six feet below the surface, nor leaped as many above it. We know not where we are" (ibid.).

In the end, the universe is still wider than our views of it. The only proper modus vivendi et operandi, as far as Thoreau is concerned, is to be outwardbound—to be a vagabond destined to vagrancy, practicing extra vagance forever.

140

September mood

In the old days, when I had to go back to work in Chicago, shutting down the cabin was a melancholy ritual. I would turn off the refrigerator and prepare myself for the deluge of cold water I'd find the next morning in the so-called dehydrator. It took me a week of days to prepare myself to leave. The cabin itself could be made ready in a morning or two, but I'd putz around—as my father would have said—in a benumbed state very much like the condition of mourning. So much would have to be left behind! Breathing, for example. What was the point of breathing in a city of the flatlands? I would therefore postpone that activity until my return in the winter.

Closing and bolting the shutters—that was the worst part of it. It was a kind of enucleation, depriving the cabin of its seeing eyes, condemning it to the inner dark. Vacuuming the floors in every room—that was the best part, and it made me wish I had done it weeks earlier so that I could have enjoyed the tidiness instead of abandoning it now to no one at all.

The wood had been sawed and chopped and stacked, the woodpile protected from the weather. Dry pine would welcome me in December, and that is precisely the sort of warm welcome I'd need. My meager spice garden and some newly acquired roses were holding on; indeed, they were flourishing, but I could see that they were jittery. Even on a sunny September afternoon, they could sense what was coming.

What I had to leave behind, apart from air and water and silence and conversations with Thoreau and Marlonbrando, was the writing. Once I was caught up in the rat race of academic life, I'd have no time either to read or to write. It is interesting to observe that what used to be centers of learning are now all about higher forms of illiteracy. The Germans use the word *Hektik* as a noun, but we in the States need the word more than they do. It names the frantic pace of our frenetic lives, such that all we can do is meet short-term objectives, meet them breathlessly and without thought. I knew that entire afternoons at the university would be taken up with bootless blather about assessment and outcomes and accountability, along with a few new clichés the administrators and professional educators had been dreaming up during my absence to make their lives seem important rather than merely hectic. Here, however, is where Thoreau is right—always was right and always will be right. We fritter away our time when we pursue those short-term objectives at our place of work. Life *is* so dear. When I am whisked away from it, I will be grateful for the hours I spent in a reading chair, at the writing table, and in a warm, companionable bed; I will rue the afternoons wasted on the puffed-up trivialities in which so many find their distraction and their salvation. That is how I assess my own outcome.

How the reader assesses it is an important question for me, to be sure; yet how much more important it is for the readers themselves! If it has been a frustrating and fruitless frittering of time for them in these pages, let us both hang our heads in shame, me for the writing, them for the reading. If an occasional thought or vision and an intermittent dream or chuckle rose to meet us along the way, well then, as my mother used to say—my mother, who had perfect grammar—

—We done good.

141

Periwinkle and ivy

The cabin is built on a kind of natural ledge of the mountain. Over the lip of that ledge, growing uphill and sending out shoots that reach toward the base of the cabin, are periwinkle (*Vinca*) and ivy. Both are evergreen, as shiny in December as they are in June. The periwinkle sprouts lavender pinwheel or windmill blossoms in spring and early summer. One or two blooms will still be there in December, along with a few Johnny-come-lately violets, as incredible as that sounds.

Periwinkle and ivy are my lawn, which no landscape architect could have designed so well. They creep over the lip of the ledge, coming to a soft end at the path that communicates between the cabin's east and west walls. Not that you ever step on the ivy, crushing it and forcing it to retreat; it just seems to know where to stop, its tender terminal triangular

leaves having mastered the art of discretion, and at such an early age! The periwinkle too desists from trespassing and concentrates instead on filling the available space on the ledge: she makes certain that there are no bald patches on her and ivy's perfect lawn. I often sit beside this plush carpet when I write, hoping my prose will weave as complete a tale, as rich a texture, as pristine a surface over the humid earth. And since periwinkle is *Vinca*, and *Vinca* a name for an ancient civilization in the Balkans, older than the Sumerian, a civilization that is said to have invented a complex system of writing, then perhaps the periwinkle around the cabin issues a call to me. Imagine writing like periwinkle, producing windmills across the page that readers can tilt at, or like ivy, patiently overcoming all the challenges with garlands of green grace! That's too much alliteration, I know, it's a fault, but who can compete with periwinkle and ivy?

142

To see and say it all

In my final days and hours at the cabin, there was always a yearning to see and say it all. It was the yearning—old-fashioned word! how silly to be using it!—to make up for the days of dulled senses and worn-out wit, days when I simply took for granted where I was, wasting the cabin's precious time. I hadn't the leisure to walk during those final days. I squatted and scribbled. The horsefly landed on my page, liked the flavor of my ink, would not be shooed, rubbed his hands with glee. He too wanted to see and say it all.

Marlonbrando sees the light

Whenever in former days I returned to the cabin after many months' absence and put on the lights, Marlonbrando was soon there on the windowsill. It took him a few minutes to notice—maybe five, maybe thirty—but he was remarkably quick to see that the Soft Touch was back. (Not that we touched more than twice, both times with me coming away with a bloodied arm and hand.) He knew that food would soon be on the sill.

How did he know what the light in the cabin meant? Or the opened shutters? It is a mystery to me still. I knew from my neighbors that he did not moon about the cabin after I left. They saw him out on the fields pursuing his life's work, not languishing on my doorstep. He was no sentimental fop. I would have worried about him if he had languished even for a day—worried about upsetting the rhythm of his life, making him somehow dependent on me. Dependent? The very word would have made him smile with quiet contempt.

The power of the past tense

By the time I was rereading and revising this collection of observations, begun more than twenty years ago, I had to emend "Marlonbrando sees the light" by placing it all, except for the title, in the past tense. It has been six years since Marlonbrando disappeared. He came every day during the long week of his demise, lying in the ivy and periwinkle beneath the July sun, eating and drinking less and less, then finally nothing at all. As he lay there, I was able to pet him—for the first time. And even then he flinched. On the day before he left for good, he barely made it to that spot in the ivy: an animal had attacked him in his weakened state—perhaps a marten or a fox—performing the sort of "cleanup" that nature is good at. I thought about trying to get him to a vet, but I could see that the damage was too severe, that he was too far gone. The next day he did not return.

I never found out where he went to die. The discretion of a cat confronting its end is so admirable! With the help of a neighbor who remembered when that gray kitten first showed up, I was able to reckon that he was twenty or twenty-one years old when he died.

As for me, I hope to hold out and to hold up here as long as I can. Last night, a neighbor woman said, over a glass of wine, that the moment she sensed the onset of Alzheimer's disease she would walk into the sea. Her husband poured cold water on that proposal.

—You won't know what the word *sea* means, or where to find it.

We all laughed. And then we were quiet.

From the mountains of Sankt Ulrich to the prairies of Chicagoland?

Goethe, in *Wilhelm Meister's Journeyman Years*, sums it up fairly well—something he does irritatingly often: "In general, life in the mountains has something more human about it than life in the flatlands."

That is a passage I read decades ago, and I always recalled it as I was preparing to go back to work in Chicago. Things have changed a bit since my retirement and my permanent residence here in the Schwarzwald. The loneliness of life in the cabin announces itself now more often than it did back then. By February, snowed or rained in, I find myself talking to myself more often than before, and not because I am an interesting conversationalist. My telephone, now a smart phone that I am not smart enough to master, begins to look like a lifeline. My emails turn into real letters, and when I send them off, I am already hoping for a response. My children are an ocean away, and with each passing year their jobs allow them less and less time for travel. As for me, that plane trip "across the Pond," as we used to say, seems to take longer each year, and the airplane seats seem narrower and less well upholstered than they used to be. Unless it is my own upholstery that is diminishing. The temptation to give it all up and go back becomes stronger. Yet it is precisely that—a temptation—and a good boy does not surrender to temptation. Listening to the news that comes out of America these days encourages me to stay here, of course.

And then there are my friends and neighbors here, many of whom have outlived Marlonbrando. Along with the water and air that sustained him for so long.

146

Life is at bottom indestructibly powerful and pleasurable

Nietzsche wrote those words in a book about tragedy—written long before he himself touched bottom, although he was on the descent quite early in his life. He wrote those words because they revealed one half of the tragedy of our existence. The other half showed itself in the words of Silenos the Satyr, tutor to the god Dionysos. When King Midas compelled the god's tutor to say what was best for humankind, the godlike goat replied with a sneer and the following devastating words, here in Nietzsche's transliteration.

—Pathetic, ephemeral brood of toil and need, why do you do me violence, that I might tell you what it would behoove you not to know? For in ignorance of your own misery you will pass your lives with least suffering. Once one is human one can never in any way become what is most praiseworthy, and one can have no part at all in the essence of the best. The most excellent thing for all of you, taken singly and all together, men as well as women, would be—not to have been born. But the next best, once you have been born, is to die as soon as you can.

In a word: drop dead with dispatch—the tiny casket is best.

Dionysos is the god of green things—of periwinkle and ivy and the juices that drive them—and the giver of wine. The god of life assuages the pain of life, transforms the catacomb into a wine cellar. Perhaps Dionysos was not an altogether docile pupil of the cruel Silenos. In any case, whenever we touch bottom, we have only the power and pleasure of life to sustain us. When she turned eighty, my mother said,

—From here on out it is all velvet.

When she was eighty-four, and after two heart surgeries, she spoke of weariness and of wanting to slip into her older sister's bed, now her dead older sister, as she did when they were children. And yet she also refuted herself.

—Every moment of life is sweet, she said.

Those may not have been her last words, which I was not present to hear, but they were her last words to me. Life is at bottom indestructibly powerful and pleasurable.

Notes

I have used the Variorum edition of *Walden* throughout. See Henry David Thoreau, *Walden and Civil Disobedience: The Variorum Editions*, ed. Walter Harding (New York: Washington Square Press, 1968), 1–252. Harding's notes on Thoreau's text appear at 255–321. I cite *Walden* by the letter W with page number in parentheses in the body of my text. SW, with page number, refers to *Selected Writings of Ralph Waldo Emerson*, ed. William H. Gilman (New York: New American Library, 1965), which contains Emerson's eulogy, "Thoreau," at 412–29. J, with page number, refers to *The Journals of Ralph Waldo Emerson*, ed. Robert N. Linscott (New York: Modern Library, 1960).

The following notes are preceded by the *aphorism* number and title to which they pertain.

5. Ice wings

The "crystalline angels" appear at the end of the poem "De Profundis." See Georg Trakl, *Dichtungen und Briefe*, 3rd ed., eds. Walther Killy and Hans Szklenar (Salzburg: Otto Müller Verlag, 1974), 26.

18. Freaks of nature; or, lighting fires and mourning the woods

Arche-ticture, as I understand it, involves a way creating things that is more reminiscent of lovemaking than of craft or technique. See Krell, *Archeticture: Ecstasies of Space, Time, and the Human Body* (Albany: State University of New York Press, 1997).

20. Maudlin and bathetic

We probably cannot count the number of students who have sat at the synechdochal feet of M. H. Abrams, *Glossary of Literary Terms* (New York: Holt, Rinehart, and Winston, 1957), in an endless number of well-deserved editions.

22. Tell Marlonbrando your dreams, honey, and everything will be all right

"Accept me as I am," *Nehmen Sie sich meiner an*, is the plea that appears in the last of the dozens of letters Friedrich Hölderlin wrote to his mother after she had stopped writing him altogether. Nor did she ever visit him during the long period of his illness. See Hölderlin, *Sämtliche Werke und Briefe*, 3 vols., ed. Michael Knaupp (Munich: Carl Hanser Verlag, 1992), 2:957. I cite this edition as CHV throughout, with volume and page numbers. Marlonbrando closes this account of the Bloomberry bush by citing the concluding line of Trakl's "Psalm": "*Schweigsam über der Schädelstätte öffnen sich Gottes goldene Augen.*" See Trakl, *Dichtungen und Briefe*, 32.

30. A reflection on consumer society; or, a Romantic has his uses

Rainer Maria Rilke's line, "*Jetzt ist es Zeit, dass Götter aus bewohnten Dingen treten,*" appears as the first line of a poem titled, in translation, "The World Rises with You," dated Muzot, October 1925.

34. La pensée du jour

"Naughty Nietzsche" writes, in *Twilight of the Idols*, "The *aphorism*, the quip, in which I am Number One among the German masters, are the forms of 'eternity'; my ambition is to say in ten sentences what everyone else says in an entire book—or rather, does *not* say." See Friedrich Nietzsche, *Kritische Studienausgabe der Werke*, 15 vols., eds. Giorgio Colli and Mazzino Montinari (Berlin and Munich: Walter de Gruyter and Deutscher Taschenbuch Verlag, 1980), 6:153. I will refer to this edition as KSW, with volume and page, throughout. For Maurice Blanchot's "fragmentary writing," see

Blanchot, *L'Entretien infini* (Paris: Gallimard, 1969); an excellent account of this theme appears in Walter Brogan, "Broken Words: Maurice Blanchot and the Impossibility of Writing," *Comparative and Continental Philosophy*, 1.2 (2009), 181–92.

For Irigaray's own incomparable style of fragmentary writing, see virtually any or all of her recent writings.

41. Platonism and Puritanism keep us on our spiritual toes

On the hierarchy of the erect human body, from the face and head downward, through the thoracic cavity, to the gut wall and the extremities, see Leo Steinberg, *The Sexuality of Christ in Renaissance Art and in Modern Oblivion* (New York: Pantheon, 1983), 27–28, 72, and esp. 143–44. For an interesting contrast to "our spiritual toes," see Georges Bataille, "The Big Toe," in *Visions of Excess: Selected Writings, 1927–1939*, ed. and transl. Allan Stoekl (Manchester: Manchester University Press, 1985), 20–22. And if you are particularly interested in the general topic of the human body, see my *Archeticture*, ch. 4, esp. 199–200n. 7 (on Steinberg) and 145–59 (on Bataille).

46. Woodchuck Heaven

Concerning that pleasant anecdote about Thoreau's kindness toward woodchucks, Henry Seidel Canby is himself considerably less effusive than Harding. Citing an earlier biographer, Joseph Hosmer, Canby writes: ". . . he told of the woodchuck he caught in a trap, and carried two miles away rather than knock his brains out. It never returned." See Canby, *Thoreau* (Boston: Beacon Hill, 1958 [first published in 1939]), 219. For Thoreau's closest encounter with the woodchuck, see Canby, 330–32.

47. Mudslide Man

With regard to the apple-tree table invoked by Thoreau at the end of *Walden* (W 251–52), see Herman Melville, "The Apple-Tree Table; or, Original Spiritual Manifestations," in Melville, *The Piazza Tales and Other Prose Pieces, 1839–1860*, eds. Harrison Hayford et al. (Evanston and Chicago: Northwestern University Press and Newberry Library, 1987), 378–97. I will cite this volume as PT with page number. The passages from Novalis can be found in Novalis (Friedrich von Hardenberg), *Werke, Tagebücher und Briefe*, 3 vols., eds. Hans-Joachim Mähl and Richard Samuel (Munich: Carl Hanser, 1978), vol. 2, *Das philosophisch-theoretische Werk*, cited by volume and page number in the body of my text. In this same aphorism, I allude to Jacques Derrida, *Glas* (Paris: Galilée, 1974), transl. John P. Leavey, Jr., and Richard Rand (Lincoln: University of Nebraska Press, 1986). I cite no particular page here, because the glandular glottal is at full gallop everywhere in Derrida's text.

52. On jealousy and brutalization

For Nietzsche (and Aristotle) on jealousy of the dead, see the last of Nietzsche's "Five Prefaces to Five Unwritten Books" in KSW 1:788.56.

56. The two corners of Melville's smile

One of Nietzsche's poems, "Ecce Homo," published in *The Gay Science*, has this as its final line: "*Flamme bin ich sicherlich!*" See KSW 3:367. For Melville's short stories, see note 47, above. For Melville's "Cock-A-Doodle-Doo! Or, The Crowing of the Noble Cock Beneventano," see *The Piazza Tales*, 268–88. I cite both this story and Melville's "Apple-Tree Table" as PT, with page numbers, in my text. To repeat, I believe that the editor of the Variorum edition of *Walden* is right and that Melville has his inspiration for "The Apple-Tree Table" from the concluding pages of *Walden*, but I also suspect just as strongly that Thoreau's "Chanticleer" also inspired "Cock-A-Doodle-Doo!"

59. Taking the arm of an elm tree

In Emerson's notes on Thoreau, we read that Henry David is "the wood-god who solicits the wandering poet and draws him into antres vast and desarts idle." This is a paraphrase of a line from Shakespeare's *Othello* (1:3, 140). I do not know the meaning of the phrase "talking birch bark." Yet if birch twigs are used to whip schoolboys, and if the tincture of birch bark is used as a diuretic and as an aid to perspiration, I fear the worst. As for Emerson's acquaintance who loves Henry but would as soon take the arm of an elm tree, see Emerson's essay on "Love," in Emerson, *Essays*, ed. Irwin Edman (New York: Thomas Y. Crowell, 1926), 127. To repeat, that "acquaintance" is Emerson himself. For the final quotation from Emerson's "Love," which closes the aphorism by rendering praise for "the fine madman," whom I take to be Thoreau himself, see *Essays*, 127.

61. On loneliness; or, snap out of it!

The "nakedest possible plain" appears in Melville, *Pierre; or, The Ambiguities*, eds. Harrison Hayford et al. (Evanston and Chicago: Northwestern University Press and Newberry Library, 1971), 297. For Hölderlin's "Mnemosyne," often revised but never completed, see CHV 1:437.

68. Tell Marlonbrando your dreams, honey, and everything will be all right, Part Four

For the image of Marlonbrando rubbing thumb and forefinger together, demanding cash, I am indebted to the late Bill Richardson for his splendid tales of Jacques Lacan.

69. Doubling up

For the story of Ulrich and Agathe, see Robert Musil, *Der Mann ohne Eigenschaften*, ed. Adolf Frisé (Reinbek bei Hamburg: Rowohlt Verlag, 1978). For Hölderlin's analysis of tragedy, see his "Notes on Sophocles," CHV 2:309–16 and 2:369–76.

76. Henry's mom and dad

The scene with the miniature seed of humankind, Homunculus, comes at the end of the *Klassische Walpurgisnacht*, the second act of Goethe's *Faust II*, in a scene set in "A Rocky Cove of the Aegean Sea." There, a crowd of sea gods and Nereids, along with the Cabirian gods of Samothrace, Proteus, and the philosopher Thales, conspires to develop a body for the spirit of humanity, which so far exists only in a glass retort. As Thales puts it, "Till now the glass alone bestows him weight, / Yet he'd be delighted to incarnate" (ll. 8251–52). They will find a body for the seed of humankind, of course, only in the sea—the amniotic sea of Galatea and Venus Aphrodite. See J. W. von Goethe, *Faust*, ed. Erich Trunz (Munich: C.H. Beck, 1972), 250.

77. More work of mourning

For Yeats's "Among School Children," see *The Collected Poems of William Butler Yeats, Definitive Edition, with the Author's Final Revisions* (New York: Macmillan, 1956), 214. On that astonishing idea of Derrida's—that beauty is always an invitation to mourning—see his "Parergon" in Derrida, *Truth in Painting*, transl. Geoff Bennington and Ian McCleod (Chicago: University of Chicago, 1987), 15–147; see also Krell, *The Purest of Bastards* (University Park: Penn State Press, 2000), Introduction and ch. 1.

79. Old people

For the story of the age when humans and animals could speak with one another, see Plato's *Statesman*, especially 272b–d. I have written about this wonderful myth in several places; see, for example, " 'Talk to the Animals': On the Myth of Cronos in the *Statesman*," in *Plato's Animals*, eds. Jeremy Bell and Michael Naas (Bloomington: Indiana University Press, 2015), 27–39. Michael Naas, incidentally, is the friend who informed me that Plato's *Statesman* never refers to the reign of Chaos as such. *Chaos* is a word of Hesiod's, not Plato's. Plato merely refers to some primeval age, earlier than the ages of Zeus and Cronos, when the human body took shape. Plato leaves it to Goethe to fill in the details.

89. The bloody truth about trees

It is of course Benjy's sister Candace ("Caddy") who smells like trees in the rain. See the first part of William Faulkner's *The Sound and the Fury* (1931).

92. Losing the whole world

Martin Heidegger claims that among living creatures, human beings alone "shape" the world. See his 1929–30 lecture course, *The Fundamental Con-*

cepts of Metaphysics: World—Finitude—Solitude, transl. William McNeill and Nicholas Walker (Bloomington: Indiana University Press, 1995). Derrida argues that the world shaped by each human being vanishes when that person dies. He argues this in several places, most notably in the second volume of *The Beast and the Sovereign,* 2 vols., eds. Michel Lisse, Marie-Louise Mallet, and Genette Michaud, transl. Geoffrey Bennington (Chicago, IL: University of Chicago Press, 2011). But see also Derrida's remarkable set of eulogies for deceased friends. They are gathered in the book *The Work of Mourning,* eds. and transl. Pascale-Anne Brault and Michael Naas (Chicago: University of Chicago Press, 2001). The French version of their collection bears the title that I have cited in my aphorism, *Chaque fois unique—la fin du monde,* "each time unique—the end of the world." Sigmund Freud's famous thesis on successful mourning as compensatory for the survivor appears in *Mourning and Melancholy,* from the years 1915–17, in the tenth volume of his *Gesammelte Werke,* 17 vols., eds. Anna Freud et al. (London: Imago Publishing Co., Ltd., 1952), 10:428–46. For the wrenching story of the deaths of Freud's daughter Sophie and his grandson "Heinele," see Krell, *The Cudgel and the Caress: Reflections on Cruelty and Tenderness* (Albany: State University of New York Press, 2019), ch. 5, "Pulling Strings Wins No Wisdom."

100. Former inhabitants . . . of color . . . at Walden Pond

I recall Du Bois's having used the telling expression "the red stain of bastardy" in his *Souls of Black Folk* (1903), an expression that adds a new color and a fundamental dimension to his thesis on "the color line." At a time when the stupidest possible things are being said about "Critical Race Theory," Du Bois's *Souls* is perhaps the most powerful and most intelligent antidote.

101. Crooked genius, crooked rules

Zarathustra's dwarf, "the spirit of gravity," makes his superficial grumble about time in part three of *Thus Spoke Zarathustra,* "On the Vision and the Riddle": " 'Everything straight deceives,' murmured the dwarf contemptuously. 'All truth is crooked, time itself is a circle.' " The lesson seems to be that crooked rules are not to be applied cynically or contemptuously. Crooked rules are for the benevolently crooked genius alone.

128. The logic of error; or, a modest disquisition on the synthesis of being, time, and truth

On "the logic of error," see Heidegger, *Logik: Die Frage nach der Wahrheit*, Gesamtausgabe, vol. 21 (Frankfurt am Main: V. Klostermann Verlag, 1976), 187. Erhard Jacoby's painting of the brontosaurus crossing the modern highway is reproduced in C. G. Jung et al., *Der Mensch und seine Symbole* (Olten and Freiburg im Breisgau: Walter Verlag, 1968), 39.

137. The man in the moon

The words *splendor* and *mourning* conclude the first stanza of Hölderlin's poem "The Wine God," later revised and retitled "Bread and Wine." See CHV 1:314. In translation:

All around us the city is at rest; the lighted narrow streets grow still,
    And carriages, sporting flaming torches, rush by.
Well-satisfied, people head for home from the day's joys to rest,
    And profit and loss are weighed by a head that knows how to count,
Happy now to be at home; the bustling market place, empty now
    Of its grapes and flowers and all its handmade goods, is hushed.
Yet a thrum of strings sounds out there in someone's garden—perhaps
    Some lover plays there, or a lonely man remembering
Long lost friends and the time when he was young—and fountains
    Gurgle endlessly on and lend their freshness to the fragrant
Flowerbeds. Quietly in the air of dusk sound the tolling bells,
    And, to honor the hours, a watchman cries out their number.
Now too a wind stirs in the grove of trees atop the hill.
    But look! for the shadow image of our Earth, the moon,
Steals now upon us too; that enthusiast, the night, comes,
    Full of stars and certainly not much concerned about us;
The astonishing one shines, she who is a stranger to us humans
    Comes in mourning and in splendor over mountain heights.

145. From the mountains of Sankt Ulrich to the prairies of Chicagoland?

The quotation from Goethe's *Wilhelm Meisters Wanderjahre* appears in ch. 2 of that work; in the Reclam edition (Stuttgart, 1982), 26.

146. Life is at bottom indestructibly powerful and pleasurable

Nietzsche's account of Silenos the Satyr appears in several places: see KSW 1:35, where the passage I cite appears, but also 1:560 and 588 for variants. A choral passage in Sophocles' *Oedipus at Colonos* (the third stasimon, lines 1211–48) is the key source for this. Nietzsche, some scholars say, found Silenos's wisdom in fragment 6 of Aristotle's *Eudemian Ethics*. To repeat, he is more likely to have seen it first in *Oedipus at Colonos* (yes, it is the choral song Yeats translates or transmogrifies in his *Complete Poems* at 223) and perhaps first of all as the epigraph to the second volume of Hölderlin's *Hyperion*, which Nietzsche first read when he was sixteen.

***Two final notes. Marlon Brando—the man, not the cat—died soon after the present project got underway. I hope my naming a local barn cat—and feral psychotherapist—after him does the great artist honor. Finally, for a more sustained, entirely sympathetic and thought-provoking treatment of Thoreau's *Walden*, see Stanley Cavell, *The Senses of Walden* (New York: Viking Compass, 1974).

List of Illustrations